The Sweet Spot in the Chaos

Also by Jonathan Potter

House of Words
(2010)

Tulips for Elsie
(2021)

Sunrise Yin
(2022)

Sunrise Yang
(2022)

How to Move to Canada
(2024)

The Sweet Spot in the Chaos

Poems by Jonathan Potter

KORREKTIV PRESS

Seattle   Montreal   London

Copyright © 2025 Jonathan Potter
All rights reserved
Printed in the United States

For permissions and ordering information, visit:
https://korrektivpress.carrd.co

First Edition

ISBN: 978-1-962934-01-5

Library of Congress Control Number: 2025939816

For NW

The only begetter of

These syllables of love

Counted on the fingers of

My naked hand and glove

Hobbling across the page

And mumbled up above

Contents

1.

The Scene Is Set 3

Dream of the Couch 4

I Get off the Bus 5

The Creative 6

The Bailiwick of the Broken Light 7

All Eyes on the Sunrise 8

Honor Song for Death's Death 10

Then One Morning You Wake Up 11

Dark Roast 12

2.

Beyond Our Fingertips 15

Just Beyond 16

This Sky Is Like My Beloved 17

Beware 18

The Red Glow 19

You 20

The Nothing 21

The Dark Dawn 22

The Dismal Winter 24

3.

Travel Day 27

The Dawn Come Round Again 28

Tina Turner 29

Conçues pour Savourer la Vie 30

The Columbia and the Yakima 31

Waking Mornings 32

The Sun Gives Birth to Itself 33

4.

River Consolation 37

O River of My Childhood Longings Lost 38

Pink and Black and Blue 39

Sapphic Psalm 40

5.

Waiting 43

Upstream 44

Charged with Change 45

Looking East and West 46

East Pasco 47

Everything Happens 48

6.

Fogbound 51

The Morning Chill 52

America 53

A Good Day to Fly 54

7.

The Birds Were Whooping It Up 57

Montreal Winter Sunrise Scene 58

8.

Thinking Back to Playing Soccer 63

Let's Let Them Dance 64

The Rain This Morning 65

BHV6539 66

Daily Sunrise 69

The Lowly Street 70

The River and the Sky 71

The Grace of Tire Tracks 72

Their Silver Noses 73

Faced with a Gray Sky 74

9.

Like Beachcombing at Low Tide 77

Not Too Hard but Hard Enough 78

The Sunrise Mostly Hidden 80

Horizon Hidden 81

Looking 82

10.

Treading on the Tail of a Tiger 85

Waking in the Dark 86

On the Train Platform 87

This Is How 88

Sign 89

Still We Breathe 90

Moving Shadows on the Grass 92

11.

The Sweet Spot in the Chaos 95

Dream of Father Paschal and the Fries 96

I Walk Along the Canal 99

Dream of Skyboarding with Todd 100

12.

These Times We're Living In 105

Early Morning Traffic 106

Sunday Morning Coming Down 107

13.

Columbia Park 108

With Whom Am I Speaking? 110

RSVP 111

The Fire of the Earth Flames Up 112

The Coyote Fellowship 113

On the Cusp 114

One and All 116

A Flock of Words 117

The Birdsong of Day 118

14.

The Birds and I 121

The Twenty-Third Psalm 122

Sandhill Cranes in the Morning 123

Milkmaid 124

Poetry on the Great Prose Plains 125

Mom 126

15.

This Poem, for Example 129

Sunrise from My Bedroom Window 130

September Is the Month 131

The Sunrise Like a Coffee Stain 132

Dear Reader 133

This Sunrise 134

16.

Nine in the Fourth Place 137

What Time It Is Where You Are 138

A Whisper of Words 139

From Deep in the Dresser 140

Dream of the Red Tin Box 142

Blurbs 144

17.

If Tomorrow Never Comes 147

Leaves of the Last Day of June 148

I Had My Time in the Past 149

The Rain This Morning Falling 150

My Wife 151

I Woke This Morning 152

The Repetition 153

Syllabically 154

18.

Dawn Repairs the Damage 157

Snafu 158

The Globe Willow 159

Qualchan Came to See Me 160

Seattle 162

Whisky-Coloured Glow 169

Dream of Vacation Skydiving 170

19.

Long Has Winter Had Its Way 175

Dream of Jess and Sherman 176

Good Morning 179

Tugboats and Bridges and Sleepy Eyes 180

The Blue of the Sky 181

Jesus in 1920 182

Halfway to Halfway 183

Fingernail Moon 184

Ode to Ayr 185

On a Gravel Road 186

20.

Playground of the Wind 189

These Messages 190

Just When I Thought 191

Take a Deep Breath 192

On the Cable Bridge 193

Swallow Sunrise 194

A Conclave of Trees 195

Dream of the Kitchen Herb Garden 196

The Gulls Have Gathered 198

21.

Solstice Weather 201

Saturday Director's Cut 202

Dream of the Rap Star Murder Case 204

Inflation 206

22.

I Thought Back 209

I Recall My Friend 210

The Clarity and Mystery of Love 212

Dream of John Updike at the County Fair 213

Hills West Above the Fog 214

The Mississippi 215

23.

Sick Day 219

Dream of Peeing My Pants 220

Going Back to When 222

Lighthouse 223

The Parable of the Tangled Lamb 224

Houses Made of Stone 227

Sun Behind Mountains 228

Bad Blood 229

The Sky This Morning 230

24.

Something Like the Sunrise 233

This Morning Was a Long Time Ago 234

The Sun Came Out 235

My Inner Rehab Project 236

Southbound Train 237

Feverish Sky 238

Farewell Song to Summer 239

Dream of Sleep-Driving 240

The Duality 244

25.

Do You Know What It Means 247

Innocence 248

Our New Agenda 249

Sunrise in the Morning Mist 250

Common Loons 251

I Don't Exist 252

High Beams in the Rain 253

The Sunrise and I 254

26.

Manuscript 257

The Path Forward 258

My Vision Is Set Ablaze 259

A Triolet From Memory 260

Like Water and Light 261

Recalling Times I Never Knew 262

The Mind of William Butler Yeats 263

Streets Are Sheets of Ice 264

Anecdote of the Stats 265

Where You Are Flying 266

27.

The Feasts of Others 269

This Canal Is a Poet 270

A Psalm 272

The Bare Ruined Limbs 273

New Orleans 274

28.

Gongoozling Along 283

The Roof Beam Is About to Fall 284

The Collapse of Night 285

My Fifty-Ninth Birthday 286

St. Joseph's Crutches 287

Its Destiny 288

29.

Wherever My Father Went 291

Toward the Sea 292

The River Rover 293

Scraps 294

The Figgate Burn 295

The Shooter 296

There Is No Was 297

Fishing for Truth 298

30.

Clinging Like Fire 301

Hanging Fire Like an Old Suit 302

Dark Glow 303

The Sky at First Glance 304

The Burning Sky 305

New Orleans Deluge 306

Approach 308

Above a House 310

Mon Amour and I 311

Connective Tissue 312

31.

Was I the Sun or the River 315

Sunrise Wooing 316

Superior Sunrise 317

The Shade Is Pulled 318

Sunset Sonnet 319

Dog & Horse Dream 320

Children 322

The Way 324

32.

An Ordinary Day Begins 327

The Continuity of Sky 328

The Duration of the Sunrise 329

It Furthers 330

Another Year 331

My Hometown Enduring 332

33.

In Retreat from the Night 335

The One Moment 336

Montana 337

The Fog Again 338

Aquamarine Jewel Sun 339

Sunrise from the Rose 340

The Outskirts of Town at Dawn 341

Substack Haiku Sequence 342

I Recall What I Forget 344

Ragged Ridges 345

The Oratory 346

34.

I Woke in a Fit of Dark Unease 349

My First Step 350

Love Is Strong 351

Bang! Bang! the Drum! 352

Travis Laurence Naught 353

Karen Mobley 354

Chris Cook 355

Nance Van Winckel 356

35.

I Dreamt of My Father Last Night 359

This Morning's Waking 360

The Moon That Rose 361

Escape 362

The Remedy 363

Thirteen Ways of Looking at the Sunrise 364

The Sunrise on the Land Beyond 367

36.

Like the Invisible Sun 371

In the Light of the Sun's Rising 372

Road Kill 373

My Poetry 374

The Smoke from Fires All Around Us 375

Dream of the Doctor and the Mask 376

Courtside 378

37.

Each Person Is a Genius 381

Electric Lightbulb Standing in for the Sun 382

Chicago 383

Jeanie Elizabeth 390

38.

Nine Dawns 393

Do You Believe in Magic? 396

39.

As Any Animal Must Know 399

Innocent Clouds Obstruct the View 400

This Morning's Version of the Sunrise 401

The Cold Ground 402

Sunrise Behind Pines 403

The Weight of the Sky 404

40.

I Woke to My Heart Fluttering 407

A Future Sunrise Will Come 408

When Deliverance Comes 409

Variations on a Squirrel 410

Squirrel Sestina 412

The Struggle of the Sun to Rise 414

A Slit of Serious Sunrise 415

The Moon 416

41.

To Increase Is to Decrease 419

The Glory of the Sun Decreases 420

Jettisoning 421

Half the Books in My Library 422

42.

Whatever Progress I Made 425

Dream of My Daughter & My Two Cousins 426

The Unburning Bush 428

Gazing into the Suburban Fog at Sunrise 429

Sunrise Ghazal 430

43.

When I Arrived in Spokane 433

The Continental Divide 434

The Ballad of Franz and Hank 435

Dream of the Intrusive Stoner 436

Fogbound at Day's Dawn 438

44.

That Fragment Reflected 441

Dream of the Donald at Doggy Daycare 442

Acknowledgement and Resolution 445

True Affection 446

45.

When It Snowed in New Orleans 449

Refugees of Morning 450

The Struggling Sun Well-Risen 451

Dream of Mingling at a Conference 452

The Color of Morning 454

46.

The Change in the First Line 457

The Reading of the Sky 458

This Work 459

Accidental Companions 460

Spring Morning Progression 461

After Seven Days 462

I Have Known These Trees 465

I Woke in a Fog 466

47.

Catching an Early Morning Flight 469

Although I Did Make It Out of Bed 470

The Fog Refused to Lift 472

The Broken Limbs 473

Autumn River Sunrise Triptych 474

Grizzled the Morning 475

Phantom Sunrise 476

48.

My Treasure Chest of Old Journals 479

The Dig 480

Dream of Sedation 481

The Grandmother 482

The Gently Falling Rain 483

What Molecules Move 484

River Graffiti 485

The Moon This Morning 486

49.

The Great Reset 489

Courage to Radically Change 490

The Season of the Change-Up 491

Molting 492

Rain Falling on the River 493

God Is a Train Car Graffiti Artist 494

Riding Backwards on a Train 495

What Is This For? 496

50.

The Open Field 499

The Ponderosa 500

I Was a Lineman 503

In Magical Ink 504

The Glassy River 506

This River Brings Time 507

In the Beginning 508

51.

The Harbormaster 511

Dream of the Toaster & the Armed Women 512

The Mountains East of Bozeman Town 513

Dawn Came Down Like Dust 514

Six Haiku at Sunrise 515

My Nine Lives 516

There Can Be No Why 521

Shakespeare, Too 522

52.

The Moon Reflects the Unseen Sun 525

Meditation 526

The Pines 527

The Place You Find Yourself 528

Sunrise Through the Sagebrush 529

Taking the Long View 530

53.

As One Word Follows Another 533

Early This Morning 534

High Drive's Your Best Bet 536

Long-Distance Love Song 538

My Long Travel Day 541

Burns Night Revisited 542

54.

My Lady of My River Dreams 545

The Pettiness of Pathetically Underpaid Poets 546

The Border Closure 547

The Slow and Steady Sun 548

55.

The Treachery of the Sun 551

The Skies Cleared Over London 552

Inwardly Free of Sorrow 553

Manic Sapphic 554

Garrulous Serious October 555

The World Inside You 556

56.

The Sky Is Crazy With Swallows 559

Los Angeles 560

The Roulette Wheel of Life's Changes 567

Riding My Bike to the Library in the Rain 568

God Made Me a Rambling Man 573

The Days Lining Up Like Birds 574

Born to Be Borne 575

Dream of Going Back to College 576

57.

Above the River 581

The Sun Above, the Sun Below 582

Three Surreal Haiku 584

Frog's Departure 585

Sunrise on the Firth 586

58.

There May Be an Ideal Lake 589

Past the Halfway Point 590

59.

All Obstacles Dissolve in Time 593

New Orleans Sestina 594

Song to the Ocean 596

The Morning Creeps In 597

Haiku Epitaph 598

Lever du Soleil 599

Sunrise Filtered Through the Mist 600

Museum of the Eternal Now 601

Dear People of the River 602

A Windy Morning on the River 603

At Six O'Clock in the Morning 604

60.

Where Not To 607

Dream of a Bob Dylan Seminar 608

Dream of Bob Dylan Preaching 610

The Alchemy Of 612

61.

I Could Spend My Life Along the River 615

Vienna 616

Dream of Hang Gliding with My Mother 623

62.

The Dignity of the Morning 627

The Lone Wood Duck Before the Waves 628

The Squirrels 629

Sunrise Solo Sestina 630

It's Not a Matter of Flying 632

63.

Preparing for an Interview 635

The Morning Is Like a Cat 636

A Favorable Outlook 637

Near the Confluence 638

The Broken Line in the Sky 639

The Frozen River 640

64.

Nearing Completion 643

Saffron Blackberry Sunrise 644

Walking on Water, Holding Fire 645

The Blazers 646

Why 647

Dream of the Biology Speech 648

Still Asleep I Leap 654

The Horizon 655

Every Now and Then 656

The Resistance 657

Sunrise 658

About the Poet 661

A Note on the Type 663

Acknowledgements & Apologies 665

Index of Titles 667

I.

乾

The Scene Is Set

The scene is set to create
a universe from the mustard seed
of a dream I can't recall.
I opened my hand at dawn—
there it was, almost invisible.
And then I blessed it and let it fly.

Dream of the Couch

for Kerry Cleavenger

I've placed a couch across the highway
That runs past the Hanford nuclear site
In the desert between Tri-Cities and Vantage.

It's the middle of the day
And no one's around. My friend Kerry
Drives up, possibly in the old T-Bird

He bought from my folks back in the day.
He stops a few yards in front of me,
His tires straddling the center line of the road.

Kerry gets out, looking like his usual
Irascible-amiable self.
We exchange greetings.

The dream cuts to documentary-style
Info about Hanford and the Hanford Reach.
We stand there talking.

I keep looking over Kerry's shoulder,
Expecting a cop or someone traveling
To appear on the horizon.

"Shall we move this?" I say.
We move the couch
To the side of the road.

I Get off the Bus
for DeeDee Downs

I get off the bus and walk
to the park where deep down things
I can hear what sings and talks
and chirps—with fluttering wings—
music and conversation
to heal a broken nation.

I find myself beholding
the tree that's often spoken
to me gently—not scolding—
about mending what's broken
by simply being alive
and letting healing arrive.

From there I walk up a path
to a carefully tended
garden where remnants of wrath
have been plowed and upended
into a lifegiving mulch
that feeds a flowering gulch.

And then to this reflecting
pond with flowering branches
mirrored and resurrecting
winter's white avalanches
in a wedding gown of bloom
undoing the winter doom.

The Creative

The opening of the gate
may be early, may be late,
but enter, don't hesitate,
this is your time, so seize it,
grab the sunrise and squeeze it
onto your tongue to please it
like an orange ripe with juice,
like an ace against a deuce,
like a river to a moose,
like the time I kissed your lips,
like the time you spread your hips,
like the gate through which time slips
into eternity's smile,
into paradise a while
while karma deletes your file
from the server of the damned,
from the chaos of the slammed,
from the ram and ewe just lambed
giving birth to a new day,
making you light when you weigh
the odds of the color gray
turning velvety and gilt,
gold intentionally spilt
across the landscape that we built.

The Bailiwick of the Broken Light
for Richard Blaisdell

The bailiwick of the broken light
Of the morning coming hard and bright
Surrounds me and sends me down
A path to the edge of town
Where no one knows the names of
Things that once were named by love.

The trees that man misidentified,
That womankind just looked at and sighed,
Now stretch their limbs to the sky,
Reminding us we will die
And maybe have already
Whether or not we're ready.

Meanwhile my shadow tells me a joke
Whose punchline involves some other bloke
I've never met but who speaks
In rhyming couplets and seeks
An understanding in dreams
Blinded by these sunrise beams.

All Eyes on the Sunrise
for Brady Buck

Hold your power in reserve.
The real game has not begun.
Be daring but be careful
To engage or to withdraw.
All eyes on you, the sunrise,
Seamlessly starting the day.

From moment to blue moment,
The real game has not begun.
The distractions of the day
Are bound to try to trip you,
So keep your feet under you
And keep your eyes on the rise.

At matins and morning prayer,
All eyes on the risen lord,
Be daring but be careful,
Antiphons with your shadow
Guiding you to make the leap
Into the pervasive light.

You have absolute freedom
In the creative smithy
Of your desire to furrow,
To engage or to withdraw.
All eyes on me, the poet,
All ears receiving my words.

And now in this extended
Moment the sky grows brighter.
The trees' shadows elongate
Into shapes of the future.
All eyes on you, the sunrise,
Comforting me with your calm.

Here I am—not Isaiah,
Nor the least bit a prophet,
But I am ready to fly
Into that beautiful sky
Like the sun blazing the way,
Seamlessly starting the day.

Honor Song for Death's Death
for M.M. Lewis

The banner of the sunrise
in its autumnal diminishing
hoists with heavy hosannas
and a watercolor wash
its calm moment of dawning,
its broken promise of death.

The poet rises from bed
to examine the bent rays of light
and consider creation
of a new song to the dawn,
an elegy for the night,
an honor song for death's death.

The poet takes a deep breath
and a long piss in the orange light
of the back yard, the neighbors
none the wiser, the new world
creating new harmonies
at the poet's blest behest.

The sun rises on its own
funeral with glad wings and tall tales
in its long, lingering train.
And then the poet sits down
to write his poem in the
unfading light of the night.

Then One Morning You Wake Up
for Jean Scheid

Then one morning you wake up
to birdsong in the garden
outside your window, and light
streaming into a swept-clean
space of possibility
waiting for your thoughts and dreams.

You feel buoyant and awake,
as though the mountain ranges
of the world sprawled at your feet,
and the oceans splashed blessings
on your brow, and cedar trees
grew in your yard overnight.

And the meaning of it all
is that you have the makings
of the realization
within your grasp, of the real,
like the handle of a hasp
of a window to unlock.

And time itself is your friend,
extending a hand to you
to bring a flowing flower
of love with humble power
into the palm of your hand
if you'll only accept it.

Dark Roast

sunrise lasts all day
in the northern climes
this time of year as solstice

approaches like a cup of
coffee you forgot
you already drank

2.

坤

Beyond Our Fingertips

Receptive thanksgiving
comes to me unfathomably
when I get up for the sunrise
climbing with the first frost
of fall framing my fear
these frail stars fading with the dawn.

The broken tree reaching
out to the river with unseen
roots delving the healing power
of the sun in the dirt
and the breeze's music
hushing winter's threats in my ears.

How can I fathom you
standing here next to me my love
with our hands reaching for the same
swallows sailing away
beyond our fingertips
into the music of the south.

How can I begin to
continue giving you my thanks
and receiving your melodies
to heal my maladies
as the autumn breezes
bring sunrises to the winter.

Just Beyond
for Dick Whyte

The tipping point of dawn
like a boomerang returning
but flying just beyond
the reach of your outstretched fingers
as the morning proceeds
in unostentatious yellow,

the bright hem of a dark
skirt of clouds above the eastern
horizon concealing
credit for the accomplishment
and only reveling
humbly in the golden changing

of the night into day,
of the day into many days,
of the summer season
suddenly into awareness,
of yellow autumn
coming to cool and calm your dreams,

prepare you for winter.
And the long dark of the distant
sun like that boomerang
then having sailed infinitely
far. And a pendulum
that inevitably returns

This Sky Is Like My Beloved

This sky is like my beloved,
receptive to my every move
even as she moves through her own

beautiful moments moment by
beautiful moment and graces
me like this everchanging sky.

Beware

for Lynne Olmos

The sun like a powerful mare—
no need for chariot or whip.
The sunrise of its own accord

happens without any planning.
Your only task is to receive
her blessings and beware.

The Red Glow
for Rebecca Gilbert

Watch for foreboding signs
As you move in stillness.
Embrace humility
And stand with calm firmness.
Align with creative power;
Clarify boundaries.

The red glow announcing
The coming of the sun
This morning like a red
Carpet from the morning
To the day waiting to unfurl.
When I saw it, something

Shifted within me, like
A clutch pedal being
Pressed on a downhill slope,
And my heart began to
Glide without effort into the
Beautiful eternal.

You

Primal power of the shadows
kissing light's reflection
among the waves brings calm,
no blame, no praise, nothing
but the reality of you
filling up the sky of my mind.

The Nothing

let the gray sky be
the nothing that you
and i are that gives rise to

the everything we enjoy
playing at being
in the golden light

The Dark Dawn

The stirring in my heart I felt
this morning stirred me to
wakefulness in the dim
light of the pre-sunrise dawn.
I rolled over on my back
and touched my neck to check my

pulse, wondering about my
family history felt
in the mirror and the back
of my mind, pointing me to
an image of the dark dawn,
a liaison with death's dim

grim grin looking back at my dim
reflection blinding my
dilated pupils' pre-dawn
shuffling walk I felt
was needed in order to
pee before going back

to bed to touch the lovely back
of my lover in the dim
calm of our marriage bed, to
sleep a little more in my
great good fortune deeply felt,
then to rise with her at dawn.

"How very early comes the dawn
this time of year." And I say back,
"How early and late I've felt
our love refuse to grow dim."
And she says, "I will come with you, my
lovely poet." "I'd love you to,"

I say. We get in the car to
go to the river where the dawn
is overlaid with all our
past and future going back
to our dreams and memories' dim
and vivid images first felt

when we felt the river flow to
the dim majesty of the dawn—
our going and our coming back.

The Dismal Winter

for Stéphane Granger

the dismal winter
can be a secret
delight when the fog settles

and an inner warmth rises
from the deepest roots
to the highest limbs

3.

屯

Travel Day
for Sea Change

The first light of day was red
spread out against the dawn
with gold and tangerine and blue
hues above the airport.
I took the difficulties
of the day in stride and waited

to depart—hesitated
when I saw the guitar
offered up by the airport bar
for anyone to play,
and so I did, tuning it
first and then strumming a few chords.

The dregs of disappointment
lingered in my fingers,
but I let them do what they knew
how to do and relaxed
into the rhythm of dawn,
into the inhale of a yawn

and then the sigh of release,
the sight of distant geese—
opening myself to invite
awareness of the light
surrounding me to offer
something strange round every corner.

The Dawn Come Round Again

I'm back at the old canal
waiting for the sunrise
to sneak its way through the lovely
chaos of clouds making
the beginning of the day
difficult and fascinating.

The sap of my veins hasn't
dried up quite yet. Summer
still has some blood flowing in it,
and before it's over
I'll break open the sky's lock
to unroll its red carpet.

The canal will continue
to flow a while longer
from its river source far upstream
until they shut it off
and let the sprinklers run dry
and the backyard gardens wither.

Until then, I continue
to wait for the promised
information behind the clouds,
for a clearing of sky
where you and I will happen
upon the dawn come round again.

Tina Turner

for Dee & John Rodgers

We begin with the sunrise
piercing the window glass
of the bilingual terminal.
So much is difficult
that extra difficulty
at the start is easy to miss.

The thing to do is to wait.
We wait for the late flight.
We wait for the Thunderdome fight
in the in-flight movie:
Tina Turner standing in
for Harris kicking the clown's ass,

my inner Mad Max waiting
to rumble with the next
patriotic idiot to
appear in the comments.
We wait for the great debate
coming tonight, all eyes on deck.

But beyond the Thunderdome
we wait for sanity
to save us from a Mad Max world.
I personally wait
for a message from on high,
for a safe flight and smooth landing.

Conçues pour Savourer la Vie

Driving down the street as Monday dawned
Behind a truck "designed to enjoy life"
I squinted as the world before me yawned

And winter kinged me where I felt I'd pawned
My hope of springtime with the queen my wife
Driving down the street as Monday dawned

And Tuesday became Friday getting conned
By Wednesday brandishing a sharpened knife
I squinted at as Thursday before me yawned

And Sunday held onto Saturday like a blonde
Ex-girlfriend who'd caused some mental strife
Driving down the street as Monday dawned

Upon my mind as on a frozen pond
Where I saw fish alive and swimming rife
That squinted as the world before them yawned

And me above them with my magic wand,
Not sitting in my car without belief,
Not driving down the street as Monday dawned,
Just squinting as the world before me yawned.

The Columbia and the Yakima
for Mikki Scheid

Burnt sagebrush hilltop
sunrise vantage point—
behold the landscape laid out,
behold the Columbia
and the Yakima
as they behold you.

As Ted said, Nature
has a thing or two
to do to you, my lovely,
so learn to go by going
down into the land—
walk gently there, friend.

River joins river
and so we also
join the flowing to the sea,
but for now we pause to see
the majestic sun
rise for you and me.

Waking Mornings

Waking mornings isn't my favorite thing to
Do but sleep reminds me too much of dying.
Rising with the sunrise, awake to something
Strangely amazing,

Eases anxious thoughts and their pounding footsteps—
Breathing with the ripples the river flows with,
Standing near the source of reality's calming
Humming-in-love song.

The Sun Gives Birth to Itself
for LeeAnn Pickrell

the sun gives birth to itself
be like the birds waiting
for the day to reveal its path

take a deep breath and suspend your
belief and your disbelief
in the certainty of beauty

Trial by Freezing
for Helen Edinger & Kate Gustafson

trial by freezing
in the aching dawn
extremities growing numb
frozen finger frozen thumb
still i write with them
bon hiver mes amis

4.

蒙

River Consolation

for Todd Curtis (in memoriam)

this river was my
consolation when
i suffered the desert of

those days of youthful yearning
and nothing has changed
now that i am old

O River of My Childhood Longings Lost
for Pamela Leavey, after Wordsworth

O river of my childhood longings lost,
The sunrise of my youth now gone,
Where clouds have crossed
The skyline of my daily dawn.
And yet the glory and the freshness still
Remain in what I want and wish and will.

Pink and Black and Blue

for Rebecca & Curran Dempsey

pink and black and blue
above an orange
and faintly yellow cavern

of emerging memory
in the present tense
of the distant past

Sapphic Psalm

for Emily Skulmoski

Walking into circles of light, the yellow,
White, and blending brightness that pulls me on, I
Find my way by my own persistent striding,
     Kicking the darkness

Dust-like under footsteps uncounted by the
Countess Killjoy kissing my feet with poison
Lips and bloody tongue and those teeth that try to
     Lacerate morning.

Pay no heed to darkening dying valleys.
I shall fear no evil nor harm from such a
False phantasm. Glory and wonder follow
     Laughing and singing,

Midnight sun illuminates where I'm going,
Banquet tables under the strain of breakfast
Bend and bow with cups running over, flowing
     Down to the river.

5.

需

Waiting

Waiting for the sun to rise,
waiting for the ice to melt,
I look in my mistress' eyes,
the winning hand I've been dealt,
and consider all my lies
and all the truth that I have felt.

Standing here out in the cold,
my bones ache to have to wait
for things that have been foretold
like free will and the chance of fate,
like the train or getting old,
like the sunrise or love and hate.

Wait I do and wait I will
for my print job at the shop,
for time to come, time to kill,
time to climb aboard, time to hop,
time to run right up the hill
to count my heartbeats till they stop.

When they do, what will I be?
You wait for me, I for you,
but in the end are we free
or are we merely black and blue,
blissful in our misery
as the sun rises right on cue?

Upstream

On top of Hills West, I wait
for sunrise like the river.
I stand still in my flowing.

You and I have been waiting in
love's revery upstream from
each other, waiting to arrive.

Charged with Change
for Ielleen Miller

The sunrise comes in its own good time
over the mountains and through
the black and blue and white clouds of dawn.

The air is charged with change—
Try to ride out the uncertainty.
Sip your coffee and be at peace.

Looking East and West
for Lana Phillips

looking east and west
i see birds and clouds
i see pavement and bridges

i see the suggestion of
sunrise and blue skies
what is it i see

East Pasco

for Tommy & Cindy Carroll

Near where the Snake crawls over dams
Into the Columbia before the great
Sweeping turn towards the log jams

Of the West as the Columbia slams
Its way through beauty under skies of slate
Carrying cargo ships and telegrams

And cohos, sockeyes, pinks, and chums
Along with sturgeons, hard to plate,
And steelhead, trout, all good with yams,

To follow up with a few wee drams
Of rye in my coffee, I sit and wait
For the clouds that cover the sky like shams

To clear a moment, with my dreams
Of summers past and winters late,
Near where the Snake crawls over dams,
With sunrise logs and sunset jams.

Everything Happens
for Julie & Michael Penley

everything happens
in the middle of
the air where we're all falling
believing that we're flying
with our broken wings
waiting for the train

6.

訟

Fogbound

I challenged my competitive friend to a contest
to see who could maintain the longest
losing streak in the game of Wordle.

He seemed confused. Do you think you could
do it? I asked. Intentionally try to lose?
I can't lose on purpose, he said. But I will

keep track of my longest losing streak!
You're still not getting it, I said.
You won't lose if you don't try.

I'm going to have that printed
on a bumper sticker, I said. My
competitive friend just laughed.

Then I stepped outside and peered through
the fog for evidence of the sunrise.

The Morning Chill

for John Hauptmann

The morning chill up on Peet's Hill
Is tempered by the rising sun
That comes up like a loaded gun
Looking for some game to kill
Or maybe just a warming thrill
Down where the rabbits shun
The morning chill.

A silhouetted figure will
Appear to be most anyone
You wish it were when day is done,
But in the early light it's still
The morning chill.

America

This great dumb land
Spicy and bland
Is fraught with wealth
On every hand

Land of my birth
A big chunk of earth
Wallowing in
Sorrow and mirth

And virtue and sin
And truth and spin
And Musk and Trump
So empty within

Two-hundred-year slump
A trip to the dump
The best and the worst
In need of an ump

America first
Is America last
For the first shall be canned
And America cursed

A Good Day to Fly
for Brian Warn

The morning of my
travel day I look
outside to see what the sky

portends for flying machines.
A glimmer of sun
seems to say, Let's fly.

Even better luck,
a pileated
woodpecker arrives as if

to say, Today you might die,
but even so it's
a good day to fly.

7.

師

The Birds Were Whooping It Up

In my dream just after sleep came,
The birds were whooping it up
outside, interrupting our sleep.

But in fact, we had drifted off
to the solidarity and
discipline of sleep till sunrise.

Montreal Winter Sunrise Scene

for Morgan Waters

1.
Perfect tree, winter foreground,
other trees withstanding cold,
bare of leaves. Streetlamps, old snow
pushed into streetside mountains,
a gas station there, and cars,
then the winter-resisting
gold-mauve-rose sunrise background.

2.
Pull back from the street and see
a bus-stop there, cold humans,
their backs turned to the glory
of the first sunrise we've seen
in many a dark cold day,
they shiver there with no time
for beauty, only to be.

3.
What is this frozen river
doing here and the sunrise
casting the shadows of trees
across the refrozen snow?
Those bare branches' dormant buds
deep within nevertheless
catch sun and slightly quiver.

4.
Early morning arrival
descending into sunrise,
bearing passengers who wish
they were going somewhere warm
instead of landing on this
frozen island with their hope
of mere basic survival.

5.
From the yacht club, Saint Joachim
and the convent seem to inch
toward the sun out on the
frozen Saint Lawrence Seaway
where Cartier and company
thought they'd followed the sunrise
around the globe to Lachine.

6.
The sun's golden stepping stones
across the ice invite us
to walk to the golden room
of our waking winter dreams
where the buds of spring are formed
in secretly fired forges
burning autumn leaves and bones.

7.
This window on the sunrise
has opened for the morning
but will soon close and pitch us
back into winter like the
groundhog's shadow retreating
into total darkness to
wait for some pleasant surprise.

8.

比

Thinking Back to Playing Soccer
for Brian Houston

thinking back to playing soccer
around the time of an
eclipse and getting sick

around that time as well
my team was undefeated
and i was like the sun

Let's Let Them Dance

for David Mock

The tipping point cannot be seen.
But Candlemas and Groundhog Day
Are lurking in the calendar.
The shadows that we live with now
Are the ones we carry inside.
My shadow and yours, side by side.
Let's let them dance, is what I say.
Embrace the darkness of the day.

The Rain This Morning

The rain this morning came and went.
In dark it fell on fallen snow.
It fell as I drove in lament:
The rain this morning came and went.
As I drove round the town and spent
Insomnia's faint sunrise glow,
The rain this morning came and went.
In dark it fell on fallen snow.

BHV6539

I got up early this morning,
Even earlier than usual,
And consulted the oracle of my phone

To see what it might foretell
About the day ahead and the night
Now floating in stillness around me.

The phone had little to say,
But the night had the moon
Like a searchlight declaring

The end of frantic searching as it sunk
Towards the western hills,
Bright and stunning without question.

I accepted a task delivered to me
By an unfeeling algorithm to drive
Two miles to a Starbucks and, irrationally,

Pick up two iced beverages at five-thirty a.m.
And deliver them seven miles
Through the dark to a hotel

Nestled near the river a mere quarter-mile
From yet another Starbucks.
None of my concern, I told myself

As I found the elevator and ascended
To the third floor, Room 314
With a Do Not Disturb sign dangling.

My little mission completed, I helped
Myself to a cup of hotel coffee labeled Bold,
Added some cream, and continued

Out into the night gradually becoming
More like the morning I was hoping for,
The moon now waving goodbye

As it slipped behind Rattlesnake Mountain.
I sat in my car and wondered if
The algorithm had any better ideas

For my next move. In silence I sat there
A few minutes, the sky faintly
Beginning to lighten. And then,

Feeling pity for the commuters
Emerging into the workday world,
I started my motor and joined the flow

Of headlights and taillights
Streaming from strange dreams
Fading into forgetfulness

And facing the need to earn a living.
I ignored the next two paltry opportunities
The algorithm threw my way

And found myself drifting along
Through Columbia Park, beside the river—
The Columbia River, mighty and deep

With memories of generations
Of spawning salmon and giant sturgeon
And the sky kissing its mirrored face.

Even now, a half hour before
My phone told me the sun would be rising,
Everything had changed.

I reveled in that drive, feeling the river
Telling me a thousand stories at once
And foretelling a thousand more.

I arrived at the Cable Bridge, an unheralded
And under-appreciated work of art
Connecting the humblest parts of the towns

Of Kennewick and Pasco like a secret
Shared between them and kept
From the rest of us—except for the poets.

As I often do, I parked on the Pasco side.
There was a cop lurking in the shadows nearby
And I wondered if he'd run my plates

As he watched me walk towards the bridge,
As I took in the sunrise in loving revery,
As I wrote this poem for you, my love.

Daily Sunrise
for rena

when i invented
this breathing moment
i didn't reserve all rights

instead i acknowledged you
as my co-author
you and everyone

The Lowly Street
for Levi Hanson

The lowly street that I drove down
With groceries from across the town,
Delivering for little pay
To someone at the dawn of day
Was somewhat black and somewhat brown

And somewhat white with winter's gown
Thrown across a bridal frown.
But still I thought it rather gay,
The lowly street.

"No Outlet," said a yellow noun,
The verb implied and you could drown
If you continued down that way
To where the river has its say.
And still I think this is my crown:
The lowly street.

The River and the Sky
for Kurt Olson

the river and the sky
are divided by
a thin margin of the skin

of a horizon and in
the river the sky
appears by and by

The Grace of Tire Tracks
for Tim Garrison

the grace of tire tracks
in the snow and the
loveliness of slush melting

and refreezing in the empty
canal this morning
the gift of the fog

Their Silver Noses
for Amber Potter

blue velvet wound of the sky
where the sun tries to bleed through
and beings of ice look up
pointing their silver noses
towards the gray liqueur of
the freezing flowing river
making its way to the sea

Faced with a Gray Sky
for Scott Nicks

faced with a gray sky
i stand a moment
at the dull tip of a point

sticking out in the morning
into the river's
melting and flowing

9.

小畜

Like Beachcombing at Low Tide
for Rick Potter

Like beachcombing at low tide
I survey the path ahead for
Creatures left over from the

Dreams that troubled my sleep last night
While I wait for the tide to
Turn and the wind to fill my sails

Not Too Hard but Hard Enough
for Mark Ward

I woke from a dream in which I punched
my estranged former friend in the face,
not too hard but hard enough to get
his attention after he'd ignored
my other attempts and entreaties,

and another dream in which a famous
writer I know was driving through
my neighborhood in an old van
gathering material for his next
bestselling novel and waved at me.

I woke from those dreams and got up,
intentionally too early, thinking
I'd try for a power nap later today
to make up for it, slid into some clothes,
descended the stairs from my room,

and let the dog out. He saw a suspicious
figure ambling through the dark
on the other side of the empty canal,
and warned whoever it was that our place
was protected by a ferocious beast.

I let him back in, made some coffee,
and headed out into the wind
that came this morning on the heels
of yesterday's atmospheric river of rain.
I drove up to Hills West and there

the wind was so strong my glasses
flew off my face and I had to cinch
my hoodie and hunch over
as I climbed up the trail for
a better view of the sunrise.

The sunrise over the hills
and the rivers of the Columbia Basin
spread out its arms of light
to gather everyone in in the wind,
me and you and everyone, my friend.

The Sunrise Mostly Hidden
for Jess Walter

The sunrise mostly hidden
Still rewards gentle patience
Standing at the river's edge

The velvet heads of waterfowl
And their marvelous feathers
Play against the golden light

Horizon Hidden

for Tali Sarnetzky

horizon hidden
by what's near at hand
branches and leaves and buildings

but still the sunrise finds you
in the morning chill
to wake and warm you

Looking

for Kathleen Brereton

I'm looking out the window at the gray sky.
It's been this way ever since I know not when.
The leaves on the limbs of the trees in the yard
Sway in the breeze and wait calmly for the sun.

10.

履

Treading on the Tail of a Tiger
for Dylan Potter

Treading on the tail of a tiger
while sleepwalking can be the best way.
Much easier than when awake.
Alternatively, to paddleboard
across a lake in the summer,
my daughter, can be quite fun.

If Sensei Watts is right and it's all
a game of hide and seek, then we need
not fear treading on our own tail.
As a matter of fact, we can have
a good laugh about it in
a few trillion years, today.

If the clouds above the lake grimace
and shake like the snoring sheets of dawn
when the alarm clock of the phone
implores the sleeper to awaken,
if you are that sleeper (or
if I am) then let us rise,

you and I, even though there is no
you and no I, no lake and no sky,
but we can play along because
playing along, especially in
the morning, is good form, and
good form is half the battle.

Waking in the Dark

for Benton Harp

I wake this morning at five-
thirty-five, which is better
than the usual three
o'clock, which I attribute
to the experimental
shot of bourbon before bed.

Waking in the dark requires
treading carefully with eyes
only one-eighth open
down the hall to the bathroom.
Don't turn on the light. Sit down
so your aim won't go awry.

If possible, don't wake up
all the way. Absolutely
do not look at your phone.
Don't worry about the day
ahead nor the trouble left
behind from yesterday.

Feel your way back down the hall.
If possible, sleep some more.
If not, then just lie there
a while unhindered by thoughts.
Feel your beloved's body
next to you and simply wait.

On the Train Platform

The autumnal sun rises
suddenly so much further
to the south. If possible
make a plan to follow it
when the winter gets to be
too much to bear and you long

to create yourself anew.
But for now, accept the chill
and the creativity—
of the leaves that change and fall,
of the sun that waves goodbye
for now, planning to return.

On the train platform, you look
into the eyes of your love.
You are deep into autumn
and she is just beginning.
She guides you onto the train
With a lost spring in her step.

And then you both are moving
while sitting still in the life
you're creating together,
no matter what the weather,
no matter where you're going
or how soon the train breaks down.

This Is How
for John Martin

Adrift, the clouds communicate their love
Of movement, gliding past the rising sun
That they can see but I cannot, the waves
Of light that indicate the starting gun
Of day is firing on the eastern horizon,
And nothing I can do will change the knaves
And jerks and brilliant people I will meet
When, running out, I pass them on the street.

See, this is how I find my way to love,
To pause and see them caught in their own lives
Like busy bees scrambling from their hives,
Or dogs with thoughts of chasing down a scent,
Until they, too, arrive at something sweet
And learn to drift to where the sunrise went.

Sign

for Conrad Lautensleger

I got up as promised and went out to seek
The sunrise in the winter, gray and bleak.
The virgin snow lay on the ground
With a glaze of ice that made a sound
Like breaking teeth wherever I stepped
And on the streets the timid drivers crept
As I impatiently shimmied past them
With pity even as I cursed them,
Hastening to where I thought I might
Catch the sunrise or at least some sight
Worthy of ekphrastic explication,
Or at least thoughts of a tropical vacation.
And when I got there, I saw this sign:
"No Jumping from Bridge. $250 fine."

Still We Breathe
for Gregg Wishkoski

Sunrise through a slur of August smoke
That's hanging like dirty laundry in the east,
My early rising feeling dismal in
The early morning record-breaking heat,
I stand beside the old canal and breathe
These lines into the sprinkler-gushing air.

I lost the handle on my sleep, the air
Upstairs a heavy blanket of filtered smoke,
The AC not quite making it possible to breathe
With ease or peace, my window facing east
Only sucking in the day's heat
When I opened it to let the mosquitos in.

And yet there is the joy of words within
This surly soul of mine. I don't despair
And do in fact delight somewhat in heat
That bakes the moisture from cigars I'll smoke
This winter after enjoying the Christmas feast,
The aroma drifting out in rings I'll breathe.

But now dog days of summer's what we breathe
And images of glaciers caving in,
The polar ice caps melting west and east
As airplanes circumnavigate the air
Above us spitting out their contrail smoke
At icy altitudes above the rising heat.

So here I stand, like a runner in a heat
She finished last in, struggling to breathe
While the winner lights a Lucky smoke
And takes a victory lap, reveling in
Applause that fills the heavy August air
As missiles and tanks approaching from the East.

Good morning, friends. The wisdom of the east
Suggests reality is larger than the heat
Or cold we feel. Our egos, thin as air,
Will disappear. The black hole that we breathe
Will be the absence that we're living in
That drifts away like a puff of magic smoke.

This sunrise smoke I see there in the east
Has drifted in from fires in the heat
But still we breathe and share the blessed air.

Moving Shadows on the Grass

   The trees make moving shadows on the grass,
but through the brightened sea of air, all full
of poles and wires, the shadows seem to pull
   the trees. Steaming slices of rippled gas
   roll off abrupt metal and broken glass
found scattered over oozing roads and dull
cemented walks: the heavy coloured lull
   of flowers saddened that the spring must pass

escapes the eyes that watch through shaded light—
   forgetful eyes that don't remember seeing
   the earth recoil—remember only being
once slightly blinded by the early sight
of death walking across the sky upright,
   and for the shadows then suddenly fleeing.

II.

泰

The Sweet Spot in the Chaos
for Patris

Over the Selkirks, the sun
squeezes color as if out
of a tube of paint and smears
it across the clouded canvas
of the eastern sky. My longing
joins it in breathing harmony—

and the feeling that the earth
is above the sky, the sky
below the earth overcomes
me in the moment of pausing
between breaths, the feeling that I
am the sweet spot in the chaos

where the breathing rhythm of
the universe is revealed
to be a dance we've all joined
where no misstep is possible
in the end because every step
is after all part of the dance.

Call it a waltz if you wish
or call it a school of fish
or a murmuration of
light and cloud and mountain and tree
where we lose ourselves in love and
forget what we were frightened of.

Dream of Father Paschal and the Fries
for Paschal Cheline, OSB (in memoriam)

It's Saturday night.
I'm walking home from Wendy's,
a large to-go bag

in my hands, when whom
should I chance to meet but my
old favorite monk,

Father Paschal, who
is hurrying to vigil
mass to celebrate

it, no doubt, in his
cheerful energetic way.
It occurs to me

I haven't seen him
in a while and haven't told
him about my drift

away from the church,
my veering towards something like
Zen, and my divorce.

Perhaps I'm also
vaguely aware, in the dream,
of the odd fact that

Father Paschal is
no longer a denizen
of this world, and so

perhaps this walk is
taking place in a border
zone between this life

and the next, which is
fine; so I offer him some
fries and open the

bag to reveal two
large cartons of them nestled
beside some burgers

I'm bringing back home
for my daughters who often
resort to such fare.

"No thanks," the padre
says, seeming to straighten up
and quicken his pace.

But then the drift of
the penumbra of the warm
salty, tasty fries

seems to reach him, and
he pauses to examine them.
"Well, on second thought ..."

He plunges both hands
into the grease-stained paper
bag and pulls out two

large, lovely handfuls,
commencing with gusto to
eat as we walk on.

I Walk Along the Canal
for Tina Stolberg

I walk along the canal
By the trailer park that must
Be home to humble beauty,
Especially when the sunset
Licks the broken limbs of the day
And sings the harmony of night.

Dream of Skyboarding with Todd
for Gary & Kathleen Lodahl

For some reason I
have a new flying skateboard—
call it a skyboard—

and I'm thrilled to be
trying it for the first time.
It's a warm, sunny

morning and I take
it to a nearby schoolyard
to give it a spin.

The grass is green and
the sky is blue, with a few
clouds, and the sidewalk

is pleasantly grey.
There's no one around as I
begin my first ride.

I find it easy
and exciting, not going
too high at first, just

making a few long
sweeping arcs above the grass,
old-school skater style.

Then I get bolder
and fly up, Harry Potter like,
about fifty feet,

carving high and then
swooping down towards the ground.
It's just then that I

see my old friend Todd
standing there grinning the way
he does. (No more, though,

since in fact Todd died
a few months ago, bringing
an end to his pain.

I understand, but
wish he'd found another way.)
But now, in the dream,

he's very alive
and flashing his trademark grin
as I skyboard by

and then circle back
around for a smooth landing
right in front of him.

He suggests we try
doubling up on the board
for a tandem ride.

I say I don't think
that'll work but offer him
the skyboard to try.

In his usual
exuberant way, he flies
away in a flash,

high into the sky,
and disappears into blue
sky and white clouds.

I stand there looking
up at the sky. A stranger
comes along and stands

beside me. We both
look up, watching and waiting
for Todd to return.

12.

否

These Times We're Living In
for Monica Piasecki

These times we're living in—
the winter of humanity,
when meanness gains the upper hand—
call for an inner retreat
while we also show up where
the sun continues to rise.

Walking barefoot across
the frozen river at sunrise
is emphatically not advised,
but there are other ways to
assert a warm gesture of
civil disobedience

and quietly protest
the icy-numb stupidity
the situation would inflict,
such as greeting with a song
the increasing light of dawn
and then making your way to

a nearby coffeehouse
for a warm cup of local brew
and friendly solidarity
to espouse community,
reembracing sanity
and poetry and beauty.

Early Morning Traffic
for Kevin & Connie Loomer

Early morning traffic
under the brutal comfort of
the unangry orange and gold
sunrise, vermillion and scarlet, pale
pink and cobalt-mauve moving into
a deep and infinite blue.

Something heavy being
pulled along the unforgiving
solidity of the highway,
the driver listening to right-wing
radio conspiracy theories
and taking gulps of coffee.

A sedan with headlights
befitting five a.m. gliding
in the opposite direction
heading to the hospital to see
her dying father, listening to
the music of misery.

In this captured moment
time stands still and the sunrise sings
a song to woo the distracted
from their distractions and back into
the flowing river of love and trust
reflecting every color.

Sunday Morning Coming Down
for Jeff Smart

"Sunday Morning Coming Down"
Is how I feel and why I frown
Rising from my bed at dawn
And looking at what was once my lawn
But now is covered with a layer
Of snow that doesn't make it gayer
And over that a brittle glaze
Of ice that breaks like crème brûlées
Beneath my feet as I venture out
To seek the sunrise full of doubt.
Rhyming couplets on repeat
Are how I get out to the street,
A ribbon of ice with slush adorning
Me, the Zamboni driver of the morning.

Columbia Park

for Daniel Patrick Bromley

columbia park
stretched out in the rain
like a patient etherized

upon a table feeling
no pain as the pink
and blue fade to black

13.

同人

With Whom Am I Speaking?
for Lisa Jensen

The sun emerges from clouds
like a benediction of light.
I've climbed down a muddy path
to catch a glimpse in the after-rain
of the tentative freshness
of this end-of-August day.

With whom am I speaking? That
was a question overheard
in childhood, spoken into
the beige mouthpiece of a telephone
by my mother to someone
of unknown identity.

I ask it again into
the lush air of the still morning.
And then I open my arms
to this gathering of possible
comrades in poetic arms,
potential friends, warm with words.

May I speak your names if I
promise to pronounce and breathe them
as beautifully as air
saturated in light will allow?
May I call you up right now
only to share this blessing?

RSVP

for Christine & Aaron Lanegan

I invite you, my dear friends,
to mumble in the morning wind
with me, stumble to the ends
of all our cares, and rescind
the fears that percolated
on thin ice that we skated

in our dreams this evening past
during the power outage dark
and the storm that didn't last,
with rain to float Noah's ark,
waking to this sunrise sign,
feeling healing in the spine.

Join me here at the river,
flowing from god knows where to where
all things begin to quiver
in the particles we share
of light not satiated
in thin ice that we skated

in our dreams, collectively,
unconscious of togetherness.
You and I respectively,
risen in our otherness,
come to find that we are one
in the rising of the sun.

The Fire of the Earth Flames Up
for Tanya Robitaille

The fire of the earth flames up
in friendship with the broken sky.
The morning rearranges
the misgivings of the night
into a gentle alarm
to awaken each and all.

The Coyote Fellowship
for Martin Mc Carthy

the coyote fellowship
across the road from where i stand
calls out to the rising sun

reminding me that i am
one voice among the many
united in strange beauty

On the Cusp

for Daniel & Michele Houston

There is a strange feeling in the air
This morning, a feeling
That the sun is on the cusp
Of the horizon but hesitating,
That I too am on the cusp
Of a breakthrough to daylight.

The cars traveling on the highway
Are coming and going
Towards the sun and away
From its orange glow above the trees.
Are these my fellow pilgrims
Approaching the gates of love?
Will we arrive together?

At last, and yet also too quickly,
The sun breaks the surface
Of the day, like a creature
Coming up for a breath of fresh air—
Daily news of division
Like this canal's muddy depths.

We live together or die alone:
The message of the sun
Rising for the good of all.
This exponentially increasing
Enmity of the factions
Is a road to destruction.

My beloved said something to me
That was like the sunrise,
A light that cast strange shadows
Across the lost highways of my mind,
A brightness both blinding and
Revealing the path forward.

Would that she and I could float away
Down the canal of time
To a place of fellowship
Away from these bitter arguments
And leaders who fail to lead
And people who fail to love.

Would that we could travel together
Side by side in a car
On a long pleasant journey
To a destination, though unknown,
Without a doubt marvelous,
Happily ever after,

To find our place in the fellowship
Of the eternally
Recurring mystery of
The never-failing ebb and flow of
The rising and setting sun,
The setting and rising sun.

One and All
for Edward Moltzen

over the glassy surface
of the river rises the sun
a gentle force that unites

and synchronizes the day
one and all are invited
to join in this fellowship

A Flock of Words
for Kelly & Christopher Evans

Out into the world a flock
of words flutters to bring winged song
to the minds of the many.
There is singing and dancing
in the dark of the paved streets
brightened with many streetlights,

lined with many mysteries,
softened with many nightingales,
nested on these limbs of love,
fluttering out page by page
in the hope of the morning
in the holy dance of death,

in the libraries of love,
reading rooms of the curious,
while everyone sleeps, the churn
of paper and ink and thought
unspooling at unblinking
speeds reaching out to the many

who upon awakening
feel the thump of the newspaper,
and each sing an honor song
to the hidden fellowship
of words now defying death
at the sudden speed of light.

The Birdsong of Day

Quietly the morning crept
into the fellowship of dawn.
I don't blame you if you slept
in the bed that you lay on
while I in stealth made my way
to join the birdsong of day

down at the river with its
population of all manner
of creatures and bright spirits
absent from your day's planner
joined together in diverse
groupings of the multiverse.

The secret society
of the sunrise early risers
gathered in strange piety,
reporters and reprisers
of light on the horizon
heralding the starting gun

that would wake you from your sleep
to meet my waiting open arms.
I don't blame you if you would keep
hitting snooze on your alarms,
but now let's go together
out into the day's weather.

14.

大有

The Birds and I
for Megan Youngmee

The sky is in the river.
The sun is a ball of flame
whose arrival was announced
by an early orange swath
across the pre-dawn horizon
while most of you were sleeping.

The birds and I were up, though,
carefully weighing the odds
of our half-remembered dreams
coming true before the clock
struck twelve and the day reached nap time
following a late breakfast—

dreams of lottery tickets
hitting bullseyes of billions
or at least mega millions
and evil men cowering
away in shame or being led
to jail for lifetimes of crime

while good and decent people
are provided a living
wage for the work of living
and healthcare is provided
and the sweet music of the birds
joins with that of the poets.

The Twenty-Third Psalm
for Gwen Halaas

The generous sky spreads out
a table of righteousness
before me in the presence
of my enemies ... and friends.
The latter thankfully are far
more numerous, I wager,
and I hope to make friends of
the former by the day's end.
But for now, I stand in the
brisk air of early morning
in Spokane and accept that I
am a mere whisp of the breeze
stirring the leaves of mid-spring
on its way to summer and
autumn and on to winter,
gliding over the Selkirks,
up into Canada where my
cup can't help but run over.

Sandhill Cranes in the Morning
for Margie Cleavenger

sandhill cranes in the morning
feasting on gold and silver
stretching to the horizon

and like coins in my pocket,
i hear their strange exultations
turn into golden poems

Milkmaid

for Peter Himmelman

Supreme success of the sun
Rising like a gold nugget—
And yet with delicacy,
Modesty, humility—
In the moment of flashing forth,
Like a hit song when first heard.

For the good of all, the song
Is composed and sung and shared,
Just as the sunrise offers
Itself like heaven's udder,
Nourishing the receding night
And gracing the coming day.

And if that song catches on,
And if that day flows with milk
And honey along the path
To the promised land, then how
Am I to be anything but
The milkmaid of the morning?

Poetry on the Great Prose Plains
for Joseph O'Brien

Sunrise a horn of plenty
this morning, my soul a tree
with branches of poetry,
standing tall in gratitude
syllable after syllable,
singing down even the moon
in its white light descending
blue upon blue behind green
upon green upon greenest
green against the broiling orange.
And the Selkirks a stanza break

beyond which the great prose plains
unroll under the yellow
incandescent glow of a
porch light. And future farmers
of America read all
these poems till the cows come home
and harvest is gathered in.

Mom

I once had a mother named Mom
Who had a secret identity in Guam,
She used to take trips
To the store to get chips
And come home with a nuclear bomb.

15.

謙

This Poem, for Example

Enormous emptiness in me
makes room for your murmurations
of unrepentant swallows
between breaths of silent laughter
and swooping, with an audience
of one whose emptiness beckons

but whose mind begins to wander
the caverns of this self-same chasm,
but yes I am listening,
or at least was—mea culpa—
till I lost the thread when some bird
carried it off to make its nest.

Not so much regrets as wishing
I might have done better in life,
in general—this poem,
for example, isn't doing
so well. Should I let it drift out
into the vast vast emptiness,

a crumpled sheet of paper tossed
into the void that is myself?
But then your birds circle round
again and I'm back in tune with
patterns against the screen of clouds
and I am your humble servant.

Sunrise from My Bedroom Window
for John & Kathy, after Wordsworth

The rising sun as seen beyond and through
      My neighbor's tree, its resurrection
          For me and you
        A corrective of the insurrection
    Of time and time's unyielding loss
That strikes me now as it has not before
         Knowing what I know
          Of morning's glow
Before I dress and step outside my door.

September Is the Month
for Ellen Welcker

September is the month
When sorrows of the summer start to fade
In resignation with the shade
Increasing and the seventh, eighth, and ninth

Numeric months' rinse of absinthe
Divide with morning marmalade.
September is the month
When sorrows of the summer start to fade.

October, in position tenth,
Is waiting with its blade
To cut the stalks and make the autumn grade.
Still till the summer topples from its plinth,
September is the month.

The Sunrise Like a Coffee Stain

for Jeanne Wagner

The sunrise like a coffee stain,
The sky a spread of white and blue,
A feeling like relief from pain,
The sunrise like a coffee stain
With clouds that move along the grain
Of winter weather moving through
The sunrise like a coffee stain,
The sky a spread of white and blue.

Dear Reader

dear reader this is
your friend jonathan
reporting live from thirty

below isn't it lovely
thank you for reading
and for existing

This Sunrise

this sunrise tastes
like a fat lip
from getting punched
the night before

like an ashtray
kiss half asleep
in the early
futility

of a morning
you have to take
with tap water
and two aspirin

and this sunrise
feels like the end
of the bootcamp
of the winter

16.

豫

Nine in the Fourth Place
for Elaine & Edwin Reinking

Let go and be like these
Fir limbs in joyful disarray
Celebrating the rising sun.
They're not showing off, they're just joining
The dance that was set in motion
When the universe exploded.

Nine in the fourth place means
Gather some friends together and
Rekindle the flames of the sun
In each other's hearts as you venture
Forward in gladness towards a
Shared vision of something beyond

Yourselves and your petty
Cares and gripes and worries and fears.
See that white pickup truck down there?
That's me, with the visor down, driving
Into a new dawn. Come along
And celebrate the day with me.

What Time It Is Where You Are

Looking out my bedroom window,
Counting syllables and days till
Halfway to the spring equinox,
Not even concerning myself
With the hope of the absent sun,
Only wondering what time it is
Where you are and where we can go
To see our shadows together.

A Whisper of Words
after Hopkins

The morning waits in a whisper of words.
It has said things, arousing a soft look;
It murmurs in a breathing, like a breeze that shook
Hushed. How can it then now not summon birds?
Aspirations of flocks and schools and herds;
Awaken all who sleep; take, shake your book
And tear its pages one by one: each nook
And hook now has no sky-shield, torn in thirds.

With its first breath, morning has spoken things
That make the blackened blanket far flung dreams
Of night now cloudsoft gleams and churchbell rings
Arraying in my green grasp sunrise beams
Because the turning earth suddenly brings
Dawn's light through wide weave and through ah! torn seams.

From Deep in the Dresser
for Mike & Jamie

I woke up this morning to find not one sock
That matched a single other sock. So my left foot
Sported a white athletic one, striped in loveliness,
And my right foot a black one from deep in the dresser.
I put on underwear and pants and looked in the mirror,
Then a shirt and finally some shoes suitable for a run.

I did a dance as the coffee machine began to run
And when I took my first big slug it gave me a sock
In the brain with a caffeine punch that cracked my mirror
From top to bottom, from head to foot,
But the crack filled with gold from deep in the dresser
Creating a vision of wabi-sabi loveliness.

A beautiful day awaited me, and the loveliness
Of the sunrise greeted me as I prepared for my run.
There was just one more item from deep in the dresser
That I'd need to complete my look: another sock
To use as a headband, not to put on a foot.
I chose an orange one and again checked the mirror.

"Behold," said I, "a cracked man in a mirror."
And then I thought of your lovely loveliness
And imagined the smoothness of your naked foot
As I stepped out into the light to begin my run.
Looking down at my own feet I enjoyed how the striped sock
Mismatched the eight-ball black one from deep in the dresser.

From deep in the dresser, I say, from deep in the dresser,
Where Adam stored the dreams from Eve's mirror,
Where mysteries lurk and a portal takes one sock
After another transported in singular loveliness,
To where many mythic meanderings and musings run
Down rabbit holes when the game is afoot.

But there I was at the threshold about to step foot
Onto the street when I felt as though deep in the dresser
The sky's sunrise colors began to run
Together and the river like a magic mirror
Reflected it back into a gigantic loveliness
That ruffled in the breeze like a majestic windsock.

The happiness of my foot stepped forth in that black sock
From deep in the dresser and from there the loveliness
Of life made me run — to you and away from my mirror.

Dream of the Red Tin Box
for Simon Hunt

I'm holding a tin box
purchased at the duty free
shop in some airport,

Heathrow perhaps. It's
painted red and on one side
it has the names of

famous British fire
trucks and on the other side
the names of famous

British ambulances.
C.S. Lewis wrote about them,
perhaps invented them.

Inside the tin, as
I understand it: cards and
possibly cookies

(biscuits) for snacking
and for playing a game based
on the various

unique sirens
of the fire trucks and
ambulances.

The challenge and fun
is to know your history
as you eat your treats.

Blurbs

When I asked GK for a blurb
I worried that I might disturb
The genius at work
But he didn't shirk
Providing a blurb so superb.

And then there's that Jonathan J.
Whose blurb lit some fire to my hay
For a great conflagration
Of sweet adulation
And mythmaking making the day.

Now Ms. Wright can blurb with the best
And her blurb came last but impressed
With fantastic words
That gave flight to birds
From a Petrarchan palimpsest nest.

17.

隨

If Tomorrow Never Comes
for Joseph Renn

"If Tomorrow Never Comes"
comes on the radio as I
drive to the golden rivershore.
And the thought crosses my mind
that the memento mori
of the morning follows the night.

My beloved back in bed
has no idea I might be dead,
which makes me smile because I'm not.
And this country earnestness
is all right. Let's dwell on death
a moment and move on with life.

So I join my voice with his,
and try to wring the bathos out
of it a bit while holding on
to the darkness in the light
that's blinding me as I look
at this tomorrow as it comes.

What day it is today makes
no difference to the dying
or the dead. Alone in their beds,
the living eventually
wake up to face the risen
sun with no thought of tomorrow.

Leaves of the Last Day of June

for Stacy Pambrun Demory

Leaves of the last day of June
follow the guidance of the sun
and kiss the shadows of the clouds.
The sun rises to give up
any need to be followed.
It traverses the sky, gently.

I Had My Time in the Past
for James Wahl

I had my time in the past
and although that time is now gone
it continues to anchor
my dreams in the dark of day,
so perhaps it's time to pull
up anchor and wake to new dreams.

The Rain This Morning Falling

the rain this morning falling
on the murky glassy surface
of the canal now receiving

its fresh seasonal flowing
i feel the rain and follow
where my followers would lead me

My Wife

my wife is standing
awake and bemused
at the living room window

as i consider the sun
glowing in her hair
and the day ahead

I Woke This Morning
for Michael Muir

i woke this morning
after a good sleep
and drove down to the river

to see what kind of sunrise
the river and sky
might offer my eyes

The Repetition
for Gus Muir

the repetition
of day after day
is an opportunity

to dance to the music of
the wild strangeness of
the ordinary

Syllabically

Dylan Thomas was a fellow
who liked to write syllabically.
(Sometimes it can be difficult
to determine the number of
syllables spoken in certain
words, especially when mumbling.
But let's agree *syllabically*
does in this case consist of four.)

18.

蠱

Dawn Repairs the Damage
for Daisy Cashin

Dawn repairs the damage
done by the black cats of night.
The squirrels of the morning
playfully awaken.
They taunt the cat and flirt with death
While bags of mulch lie in wait.

Snafu

for Gregory Spatz

Our work has only just begun.
The chaos to come is real
and yet all part of the game.
Situation normal, all fucked
up—whoever came up with that—
"snafu"—a fucking genius!

And now we face the rise of a
demented, damaged dolt
who has somehow managed to
gather a cult of mesmerized
mothers against drunken driving
to ride off the cliff with him.

So, yes, there's some cleanup to do.
It isn't normal, and yet
it is, this snafu we find
ourselves in. We are the authors
of this book we're reading, this game
we're playing. The chaos to come
is real, but we have made it.

Our work begins with the sunrise.
The cleanup of the moment
is already happening.
We have our work cut out for us
to reclaim the democracy
of the ever-changing sky.

The Globe Willow

for Stanley Wotring

The globe willow was wounded in the wind,
Mortally it would seem, split down the trunk.
But a healer of trees spread some gluey gunk
Along its inward grain hoping to rescind
That death sentence with the help of a clamp
To weld its two halves together—a perfect fit.
Your mind and soul once felt that kind of split
From forces that blew out your waking lamp
Some time ago only to eventually awaken
From your own windstorm badly shaken
And nearly dead but living on to walk
Into a universe that healed you of the shock
And left you dancing towards your lovely fate
Whatever that may be—don't hesitate.

Qualchan Came to See Me

Qualchan came to see me at 9 o'clock, at 9:15 he was hung.

Left, right, bike, park only—
Is what the sign says where I've stopped to watch
The sun come up over the edge
Of the Palouse, south of Spokane where dreams
Of a Steptoe utopia formed by Ice Age floods
Combine with a hesitant pioneer spirit

That stopped well short of the oceanic spirit
To settle here where basalt cliffs are the only
Walls you'll see and the river rarely floods
Due to the dam keepers keeping watch
And the gunpowder and germs of colonial dreams
Pushing the Indians out to the town's edge.

I'm looking down from the bluffs' edge
At the creek below where Qualchan's spirit
Fistfights the spirit of Wright in my dreams
Of the morning while my ancestors are only
Keeping a European famine watch
And Coyote is drinking from Lake Missoula's floods.

The Children of the Sun soak up the floods
Of sunlight coming from the edge
Of every sunrise as the people watch
The sky for colors of trout and salmon spirit
Guiding the Ghost Dance in frigid winter's only
Possibility: to freeze the invaders in their dreams.

Qualchan came to see me in my dreams
At nine o'clock and the sun with its floods
Had long since risen. I was Wright and only
Wavered at 9:15 upon the bluff's edge
To the left of where I'd parked my bike, my spirit
Looking to see that he'd been hung, my watch

Telling me that time had stopped to watch
Eternity in the sunrise through Ponderosa dreams.
But I woke up to winter and the holy spirit
With a wind chill factor off these glacial floods
Speaking deeply to my bones from the edge
Of some other universe where the sunrise only

Could be felt, only tasted, no eyes to watch
From the edge of George Wright's dreams
And Whist-alks' floods of tears and broken spirit.

Seattle
dozzina

I find not loving you, Seattle, impossible,
Even though my earliest Seattle memory
Is of some bullies at Seattle Center
Trying to start a fight with me and my cousin
Brad when we were little kids and left
To our own devices early one summer morning;
I had knelt to tie my shoe in a leafy
Corridor between the carnival area
And the fountain — the Space Needle looming up above,
No doubt, in all its hokey splendor;
This kid was big and showing off for his cadre
Of fellow thugs when he veered to knock me over.

I was a kid from a small town way over
On the dryland side of the state and my center
Did not hold. I hit the asphalt. My cousin
Pulled me up and we skedaddled above
The taunts the bullies leveled as we left
The scene. That incident engraved some area
Of my brain perhaps with a tangle of leafy
Apprehensions mixed with a view of the splendor
Of the Emerald City; so when, with my own cadre
Of skate-punks, I went again to that impossible
City to attend the Devo concert, my memory
Tingled within me and lingered the next morning.

By then we'd moved to Kennewick where the morning
Sun often packed a punch. My cousin—
The same one—Brad—appeared one time above
The front steps having stolen a car with a cadre
Of teenage hoodlums and was in the area
Attempting to get away from Seattle to a leafy
But different place. I stood there with impossible
Thoughts stuck in my brain and that memory
From childhood blocking my sense of the splendor
I could've offered him: to stay while they left
And then personally give him a ride over
The mountains and back to Seattle Center.

Halfway through college, again I lost my center
Of gravity, my ability to calculate the area
Of my soul, and ended up in a leafy
Place north of Seattle. Due to impossible
Odds my aunt and uncle, the parents of the above
Brad, now took me in because Brad had left
For who knows where and I dropped out and came over
For a job and to surrender to Seattle's splendor.
I worked the evening shift, which is like a cousin
To the day shift and leaves the blessed morning
Free for rides on the Burke-Gilman Trail with a cadre
Of other travelers, to the U-District to heal my memory.

I spent my time applying Kierkegaard to memory
And riding my bike past joggers in the center
Of the trail. I wrote some poems on leafy
Sheets of notebook paper and ascended above
Red Square and the buskers there to the scholarly area
Of Suzzallo Library, the reading room, where in the morning
I'd pretend to be what I in fact thought impossible,
A university student and a philosopher of the splendor
Of truth and beauty, an inquirer into what was left
Of ancient mystery and its weird cousin
Postmodern possibility sizzled over
The flames of a misapprehended Kierkegaardian cadre.

I returned to college, now out of sync with my cadre
Of classmates and stacked it to reduce the time I had left,
So I could return to Seattle — the elder cousin
Of Walla Walla where I found myself every morning
Sniffing around campus and the general area
Of the town for clues from literature and memory
That would guide me to graduation and the impossible
Task of finding my fortune in post-grad splendor
On the glistening streets of Green Lake, above
Lake Union and below the Northgate shopping center.
That's where I landed somehow, going over
To a house that had a room and a view of leafy

Neighboring yards, the backyard bordering on leafy
Realms of coincidence and untold splendor
To later reveal, improbable but not impossible;
Out the front door to drive to a job with a new cadre
Of blue-collar workers in the Bellevue area
Where I was the grunt and the unfortunate center
Of the foreman's abrasive attention. He was a cousin
Of the devil and made my life miserable over and over
Day after day, so one day I got up in the morning
To find my truck had a flat tire, like a deflated memory,
And I said forget it. I'd made enough above
My savings to survive a while on what I had left.

I wandered out one night, the freeway to my left.
I went under it, the rumble of cars over
My head as my feet moved through the impossible
Motions of my mind, past the Latona and its cadre
Of evening people planning to stay out till morning
It seemed. I kept walking, creating an uphill memory
And then down towards the lake in its humble splendor
Laid out before me. I paused there high above
Everything I'd ever known and felt the center
Of my soul expand, Seattle the second cousin
Of my dreams surrounding me with the leafy
Belief that I could anchor myself in that area

And make—if not in the city, then in a nearby area—
A home for my life and a place to center
My self away from the places lacking splendor
Where I'd been formed. Unemployed, my memory
Turned around and got a job just over
The hill from there, after pawning my impossible
Dreams to pay the rent that month, the leafy
Feeling of bills leaving their last cousin
In my pocket, handed over to my cadre
Of housemates as I walked to work that morning
For a new job down the hill and to the left
From where I lived two blocks above.

So long ago, Seattle. Now above
Your crazy quilt of land and sea, of leafy
Shorelines and wooded paths I squint to center
My blurry view towards the upper left
Corner of the map, the place where a cadre
Of billionaires and baristas mull over
The tedious weather and whether the impossible
Might turn out, like the sun in surprising splendor,
Or like Mount Rainier appearing in the morning,
To be quite possible. Clouds cover the area
But there is always the blissful nagging memory
Of the return of blue sky like some lost cousin,

That supreme feng shui so like a favorite cousin
As I begin my descent down into your leafy
Streets of sometimes painful lovely memory.
But I could never not love the entire area
Of you, Seattle, your ferryboats keeping impossible
Schedules day in and day out and your cadre
Of fishmongers and booksellers, your center-
Of-attention attitude as if above
The horror of indigenous history, coffee in the morning,
Beer at night, and salmon seared over
Coals on cedar planks, your leaning to the left
In semi-oblivious sometimes-awakened splendor.

Seattle, I could never not love your splendor,
Your hills and shorelines keeping you off-center.
As I step off the plane with my memory
And the one I love, I find that I have nothing left
But the present and its every morning,
The calendar and its casually marching cadre
Of days like eggs cooked briefly and then flipped over.
I hold your hand and take you into this leafy
Place of my haunted past. We descend from above
Queen Anne hill on our bikes, the whole area
Inviting us through Fremont, past my cousin
The troll, on a journey that seems impossible.

But nothing's impossible in the aria of this area,
Seattle, its constant cadre of coffee drinkers and leafy
Creatures guiding us above the memory
Of the last hill over to Woodland Park and left
Turn as cousin of right turn leading past morning
To lunch at Duke's at the center of our splendor.

Whisky-Coloured Glow
for Douglas MacQuarrie

whiskey-coloured glow
above silvain's house
on the anniversary

of the day after the day
my dad breathed his last
and we felt the loss

Dream of Vacation Skydiving

I'm with a group of people—
family members, maybe, and
maybe on vacation somewhere—
and we're all getting ready
to go skydiving.

We're gathering on a lawn
with our instructor,
going over the process.

Someone standing next to me
(who is like my niece
but isn't my niece—or is
perhaps my niece in a parallel-reality
alternate-universe kind of way)
asks if I'm scared.

Not really, I say.

And then I picture in my mind
how it will be jumping out
of the plane—confirming to myself
that indeed I'm really not scared,
that I can handle it just fine.

The scene changes
to on board the plane.
Everyone starts putting on
their parachute packs.

As I put mine on, I notice that
(a) the straps seem a bit flimsy, and
(b) on one side of mine (the right side)
the little bracket that attaches
the strap to the chute pack
is broken.

The scene changes
and my dad (who is no doubt paying
for this experience for everyone) and I
are back at the skydiving company's
headquarters. I'm carrying
the defective chute pack.

We've been directed to the office
of the owner of the company
located at the top of a long flight
of wooden stairs on the outside
of a hangar-like blue metal building.

My dad takes the lead and I follow
up the stairs. He knocks at the door,
and an elderly, tidy and intelligent looking
Japanese gentleman opens it and invites us in.

I Hesitate to Say

I hesitate to say
what motivates these lines.
But if you insist, then
I'll tell you it's from when
I kissed your ruby lips.

19.

臨

Long Has Winter Had Its Way

for Kathleen Hobbs

Long has winter had its way
with me but now the sun is rising
on a new day that seems to say
something both old and surprising
is on its way and spring
has a mischievous plan

to light up the waiting world
and lighten in time the heavy load,
the pressure of reality
that has been pressing down on us
ever since the strange thing
happened that we can't quite

recall, back in the fog of winter
coming on, when chaos got the edge
and pulled the ground out from under
the preoccupied dancing of
our unsuspecting feet,
when life had been so sweet.

But now spring is coming on
like an invisible dervish of
resplendent opportunity
to dance with the sunrise again
and join hands with new friends
to face the joy to come.

Dream of Jess and Sherman

for Shawn Vestal & Amy Cabe

I am out walking
in my town one spring evening
when I find myself

wandering unawares
in a dream version of Jess
Walter's neighborhood.

I know where Jess lives
in real life, but in this dream
it's some other place

concocted by my
subconscious, Lord knows why, and
reminiscent of

where my friend Todd lived
in high school and where we would
go to skate or swim

or thrash guitars and drums
in some semblance of music—
the angry white kid kind.

In the dream, I am
approaching the corner where
I know Jess lives, but

first I see the house
next door, translucent windows
lit up from within

and revealing a
hi-def Sherman Alexie
calmly vacuuming.

Sherman's back is turned
but I am nevertheless
quite certain it's him.

I'm taken by this
domestic scene and surprised
and pleased to see him.

There's satisfaction
and contentment in the way
he wields the vacuum

with smooth, sweeping strokes
across the smooth hardwood floor,
like a kind of dance.

Cut to: the next day.
I run into Jess downtown
and mention my walk

and my happenstance
discovery that Sherman
is now his neighbor.

Jess smiles and nods and
we stand there chatting a while,
I trying not to

appear bedazzled
by his literary fame,
he generously

opening the door
for me as we both go in
the grocery store.

Good Morning

Wake up and say good morning to the night,
Get dressed, drink coffee, and be on your way
Across the river in the morning light.

I think of your insomnia and fight
To stay awake. I hear the coffee say,
Wake up and say good morning to the night;

The sunrise on the bridge a welcome sight
As sleep returns to you so far away
Across the river in the morning light.

I'll drive all day and then I'll catch a flight
To catch the sun and try to make it stay
Awake to say good morning to the night.

And with the runway beacons shining bright,
You'll look and see that everything's okay
Across the river in the morning light

Because the sun's the same and it is quite
Intent to have the birds who swoop and sway
Wake up and say good morning to the night
Across the river in the morning light.

Tugboats and Bridges and Sleepy Eyes
for Mills Baker

The city of New Orleans at sunrise
Awakens in a thousand different ways
With tugboats and bridges and sleepy eyes

Opening to a canvas of turquoise skies
And blinking with a dizziness that sways
The city of New Orleans at sunrise

And Bourbon Street's creative lies
About last night and the night's sashays
With tugboats and bridges and sleepy eyes

And Hurricanes and Sazeracs and Ryes
And memories of those good Big Easy days
And the city of New Orleans at sunrise

With oyster beds and pecan pies
And skirting past the traps of the malaise
With tugboats and bridges and sleepy eyes,

Binx Bolling and his girl with lovely thighs
For whom he sings nothing but her praise
In the city of New Orleans at sunrise
With tugboats and bridges and sleepy eyes.

The Blue of the Sky

for Harper Greenside

the blue of the sky
the gold of the sun
the white and the green

of the clouds and trees
and the scent of pine needles
hanging in the frozen air

Jesus in 1920

for Marc Shepherd & David Hughes

Jesus in 1920
was erected on the shore
in front of Saint Joachim
to stand there and herald the
freezing and the melting and
the seabirds celebrating
the hope of Jesus' shadow.

Halfway to Halfway
for Theo Muir

halfway to halfway
between winter and
summer no sunrise is a

good sign according to lore
no shadow's showing
and river's flowing

Fingernail Moon

for Andy Volmer

fingernail moon
rising ahead
of the sunrise
above a palm

palm trees standing
in ecstasy
perpetual
for the sunrise

riverboat waits
for coffee at
sunrise and booze
when the sun sets

mississippi
river sunrise
music echoes
big easy dreams

Ode to Ayr

The air of Ayr is fresh and spare
As I stare at my fair lady's derrière
And dare to ask her if she'll share
Her fish and chips with me
Beside the sea.

And Rabbie Burns was born here,
The result of his mother drinking a beer,
Succumbing to her husband's cheer,
And lying down so spry and free
Beside the sea.

On a Gravel Road

for Patrick Samway, SJ

on a gravel road
along a winding
irrigation ditch the sun

peeks over some scruffy trees
and brings me to my
old and well-worn knees

20.

觀

Playground of the Wind
for Angela Potter

How could the wind refuse to blow
when the earth and sky make such a
perfect playground for it, and when
contemplation takes the form of
a gentle wandering breeze
in the soft early morning?
On such a day the songs of birds
carry a wisdom without words

and the music of the river
hums in undulating whispers,
the raccoon hails the beaver,
the rabbit eyes the squirrel,
and among them I go walking,
learning from them without talking.

These Messages
for Francesca Bossert

The canal has been flowing past,
Carrying tumbleweeds of time,
Waterfowl of wonder,
And now these messages
I place in bottles with the sunrise
And send downstream to be found by you.

Just When I Thought
for Síodhna McGowan

My dreams have been resisting me,
Slipping with the sunrise into
The murky waters of
Forgetful wakefulness
Just when I thought I should have arrived
At a state of supreme consciousness.

Take a Deep Breath
for Michael Herzog

1.
Take a deep breath and let it out.
Allow it to join with
the wind softly shaking
the old fir's dangling limbs
as the dog in the yard sniffs the air,
considers barking, and stops.

2.
Take a deep breath and let it out.
The teens running and breathing
along the empty canal
are building up their hunger
for tonight's rejuvenation.
The dog, too, will eat and sleep.

On the Cable Bridge
for Richard Door

On the cable bridge,
I stopped to look
At the sun rising through a crook
In the clouded ridge

Like a smudge on a cluttered fridge
Or a cocktail I only just shook
On the cable bridge
Where I stopped to look.

For a moment I squidge
My eyes to read from this book
Of the sky, and a smidge
Of time floats down the brook
Beneath the cable bridge
Where I've stopped to look.

Swallow Sunrise

for James Maynard

The swallows, martins, gulls, and chirping wrens
pay little mind to me along the shore
where Kaniatarowanenneh bends
around the elbow of the island, more
like morning, scented with the after-rain,
than later when the sun begins to bake
the air, and future memories complain
that time is always lurking and will take
the sunrise and the morning on its way
to afternoon and evening getting dark,
the long night to have the final say,
to pluck with death the song out of the lark,
and yet again we trust another morning
will come when Alouette sings its warning.

A Conclave of Trees

for Michael Sweeney, O.P.

a conclave of trees
in the early fog
of what would be the sunrise

the trees hold their faith and turn
their backs to the street
and i stand with them

Dream of the Kitchen Herb Garden

The windstorm yesterday left the sky
a dog's breakfast of frantic clouds
hiding the sunrise this morning.

The dream I woke from before looking
out my bedroom window
was of finding myself alone

in my wife's kitchen with my mother
and my mother-in-law cheerfully
teaming up to cook and clean

and mother-hen me to within inches
of my sanity. Then (in the dream)
an email arrived from yet a third

mothering figure in my life,
my wife's elderly friend Carole,
with a bit of laundry advice.

In the dream, I jovially shared this email
with my mother and mother-in-law,
and we all had a good laugh about it.

My mother and mother-in-law resumed
their cooking and cleaning and mothering,
and I stepped, cautiously and bare-footedly,

into my wife's kitchen to survey the scene.
Looking down, I saw what I took
to be several small weeds growing

out of the cracks between the floor tiles,
and I bent down to pull one of them,
concerned that the two mothers

would be judging my wife for letting
the kitchen go to seed like that,
when I realized it was intentional.

My wife had planted an herb garden
in the cracks between the tiles
of the kitchen floor.

So I rose from my bed and looked
out the window, checked my morning
message from my beloved in Montreal

(that is to say, the aforementioned wife),
reported the dream and got a laughing
emoji and an "omg, it sounds too realistic,"

descended the stairs to the kitchen
(a different kitchen), prepared some coffee,
stepped out into the backyard,

the wind now much calmer
than yesterday, and snapped a photo
of the wildly whirling sky.

The Gulls Have Gathered

The gulls have gathered
in Lac Saint-Louis
as if occupying seats

in the auditorium
of early morning
for the sunrise show.

They've paid their tickets
and now sit and watch
the sun break the horizon,

its reflection resembling
a golden comet
rising from the depths.

And who then am I?
The unpaid usher
of the solemn occasion?

Or the human element,
mostly unheeded
by both sun and bird?

A strange intrusion
at the glazed margin
peninsula of being,

observing, but still asleep,
only opening
one eye a little.

21.

噬
嗑

Solstice Weather
for Simone Senisin

The weather is endlessly
fascinating in its changes
from the sputtering rain—
the splat of fat drops on the windshield—
to the frayed hem of cloud cover
on the golden horizon

as the days of December
dwindle down to deepest darkness
and the brisk quietness
of the expectation of the snow.
You find yourself walking along
the river with your mother

and your daughter's dog pulling
you along, leash taut and straining,
because the weather changed
from drizzling rain to solstice sun
at the end of the shortest day,
the stinging rays struggling

across the earth's curvature
to reach your face and cut across
your eyes, mercifully,
a blade of light from its furthest point
cutting the tumor of darkness
from the weather of your soul.

Saturday Director's Cut
for Toby

Cutting through disturbing dreams
To wake up this morning, I stepped
Outside and saw the sky pressed down
On the horizon and the
Trees reaching up to tickle the
Clouds, perchance to make them rain.

And so it did rain, meager
Droplets cutting through the
Layers of my thoughts to reach me
Standing there in the backyard
With my dog wondering when we
Might go for our morning walk.

And so we did, go for that
Walk, the rain coming and going,
The sky offering resistance,
My dog pulling at the leash,
My mother trailing steps behind
As we cut through the meager

Saturday reality,
The day giving way to something
We couldn't quite put finger on,
Or paw, until we turned back
Towards home and a breakfast of
Fried egg and avocado.

My wife would've cut through that
Breakfast with proper cutlery,
But my mother and I tore through
It on toast with our bare teeth—
Because we are Americans—
And the dog waited for crumbs.

And for the rest of the day
I cut through knots of employment
To unravel a few dollars,
And I considered the roses
And their thorny stems waiting to
Be further pruned for blooming.

Dream of the Rap Star Murder Case

I'm pals with a rap star
(someone like Ice Cube
but not Ice Cube)

who's accused of murder.
He's been acquitted,
or the charges have been

dropped, but he seems
to be guilty. The question
of his guilt or innocence

seems to hinge on a crude
wire bracelet or ring he wears,
fashioned from the innards

of a broken electronic device
or something like that.
At some point, well into

the intense narrative,
I take a pair of needle-
nose pliers and proceed

to gradually bend and break
the wires and remove
the crudely fashioned piece

of jewelry from his hand.
His other friends are alarmed
and he raises his eyebrows

but allows me to do it. It's unclear
whether I'm revealing his guilt
or proving his innocence.

Inflation

for Ronald Drimmel

God's eye stares into the midnight sky
of the dark universe at the bottom of my trouser pocket.
My fingers beak like an early bird
toward God's home, the worming dollar bill,
and pull it out into the blinding supermarket light.

The cash register stamps out the vowelless syllables
of His name in whom we trust.
The lovely checker is my priest and confessor,
transubstantiating the fading green
NOVUS ORDO SECLORUM ANNUIT COEPTIS
at exactly the rate of inflation.

And the Twinkies I buy today
cost a few cents more than a month ago,
but I have traded God for these Twinkies
so I know they are worth much more.

22.

貰

I Thought Back

for Randy Free (in memoriam)

I thought back to a moment
that I almost held in my hand,
that was soon gone, never to return,
the grace of that time like the dawn,
fleeting but persisting
even as I watched it go.

I Recall My Friend
for Kyle Kinney

I recall my friend
Kyle drove at high speed
down this quiet street
when he lived with us
that golden summer.

Luckily summer
Didn't catch my friend
and take him from us
to the gods of speed
for death in the street.

This very same street,
some later summer,
saw that teenage speed
can take someone's friend,
or any of us.

He was one of us.
I was on the street
that night, with no friend,
and saw the summer
disappear at speed.

Others came with speed.
There was none of us
could bring back summer
for him in the street,
brother, sister, friend.

His friend did then speed
street to street to us,
to summer's end.

The Clarity and Mystery of Love

The museum of marginally remembered memories,
A trance of drapery hung with the music of infinity,
Salubrious paperwork falling from tumultuous skies,
Your hair a bellwether to some beautiful bonfire,
Your lips the beginning of a paradise of flowers—
These are the whispers I hear in the morning
Of our waking on the last day before flying.

Making love for the first, second, and thousandth time,
The bottomless avalanche of topsy-turvy trembling,
The love of laughter and the laughter of love,
Kissing you at the behest of a street poet in the night,
The loveliness of the left and right banks of you—
These are the sparks that come to me in the dark
Till the morning surrounds us with its light.

Dream of John Updike at the County Fair

I have taken my best-loved poems down to
The county fair where I am stapling them
To a plywood display board, hoping to win
A colored ribbon.

They are written in crayon on white paper.
I get them all stapled but then realize
There are errors, so I pick up a crayon
And begin to work.

I have one more correction to make but then
John Updike steps up and begins reading them.
I'm embarrassed, so I put down the crayon
And take a step back.

John takes his time thoughtfully perusing them,
Which I find encouraging. But his face is
Expressionless, which worries me. I wonder
If I should say hello.

Hills West Above the Fog

The feelings that came to me this morning,
As I drove out of the fog. Memories,
And the vestiges of memories, that constitute
Pieces of my life still within me
Yet drifting away, fading in and
Fading out. Dear sweet dreadful life.

The fog so settled around my neighborhood,
So insistent and persistent and intransigent,
But only a short drive in my trusty car
Took me out of it and, in a way,
Out of myself, and in another way,
Deeper into myself, to see the sunrise.

The air at the top of Hills West
Brisk, just brisk enough to be bracing,
And, blessedly, not another soul
Around, just me wearing a hat
And playing the part of poet to myself,
To myself, whoever that is, playing my part.

And the sun and the clouds and one bird
On a branch about fifty paces down
The hillside all playing their parts, too,
In this early morning of Mardi Gras,
A holiday I don't mind observing
With my own parade and masque

Within my own mind, only
Sharing it with you my secret friend,
Dear reader. So let us feel the cold,
Clean air and the ashes under our feet
From the brushfires of summers past
As we dance to the music of the rising

And prepare to give up whatever we must,
The future, the past, these memories,
Even as they do their own dance
Across this beautiful changing horizon
Of our lonely and beautiful lives
Before the business of the day begins.

The Mississippi

the mississippi
winds its way between
lake pontchartrain and the dawn
and its glistening mists
are the ghosts of dreams
welcoming the sun

23.

剝

Sick Day

My orangutan tongue like a vestige of Bornean rain
In the mouth of my mind thick with mucus and moldering rind
In the middle of morning my chest with its treasure of phlegm
I present my adornments poetically rancid and strained
Through the Indian summer its music a murmuring mulch
With the rhythms of Rilke and Auden's intelligent ghosts
That inhabit my eyelids like flocks of strange birds in the dawn
To convey this alert to imply my intent to ascribe
To the dawn disappointments unfathomed by nightmares untold.

So I'm calling in sick just to tell you I'm not feeling well.
At the sound of the tone in the jungle my fever has wrung
These few droplets of sweat from the drooping malarial moon
And my rational faculties left me a sweet goodbye note
That I read in the back of the rickety hospital bus
As I drifted to sleep and began to remember my life.

Dream of Peeing My Pants

I'm driving a scenic byway
somewhere in the North Cascades.
Somewhere off the main freeway.

I'm nearly out of gas
and feeling a little worried
about finding a gas station.

There's a small town nearby
and I hope it has one
but for some reason I decide

to pull over on the outskirts
of town where there's a siding
in a wooded area.

I walk the half-mile or so
to the town, keeping a lookout
for a gas station. (The logic

of why I'm doing this on foot
fails me now as I write this
but maybe it has something to do

with not wanting to be seen
as a city slicker too abruptly
entering the town.)

I do indeed locate a gas station
and make the discovery—
a pleasantly surprising one—

that gas is only forty-eight
cents per gallon. Suddenly
I realize I need to pee.

There's a restroom in a kind of
trailer behind the gas station.
It's tiny, like an airplane toilet

but with an even lower ceiling.
I step inside and as I stoop
and fumble with my fly

I lose control and pee in my pants.
A little. I don't think it's a lot.
But when I look down to inspect,

It's quite visible: a wet spot
the size of my fist on the front
of my light kaki shorts.

I finish peeing, without
further wetting myself,
and then ponder going back

to my car and whether
I have something
to change into.

Going Back to When

for Walker Percy (in memoriam)

going back to when
there was no language
no words only blank darkness

nothing felt anything then
the time before time
that's where we're headed

Lighthouse
for Robert Court

That winter I spent teaching
English 101 at a community
college on the coast, there was

no lighthouse to warn me
of the rocks of loneliness,
no light in the house

where I lived, just me in the dark
trying to strike a spark
with the flint of a pencil.

The Parable of the Tangled Lamb

The lamb was tangled
in the soccer goal netting
behind the house where

a hole in the fence
had let the sheep wander in
to graze on the lawn

from the adjacent
pastureland of Kilmichael.
My wife and stepson

and I were in the
churchyard next door perusing
tombstones among which

some were dated to
the medieval period.
My wife the lovely

archaeologist
was enthusiastically
scraping off the moss

and snapping photos
while I pondered possible
ancestral surnames

from more recent ones,
wondering if McIntyre,
John and Margaret,

could be my kin, based
on my father's research on
our family tree.

Just then my stepson,
looking over the stone wall,
pointed out the lamb,

quite entangled and
looking like it might strangle
itself in struggle,

bleating to raise the
dead. Tom and I raced over,
first knocked at the door,

then, no one answering,
circled around to the back
to come to the aid

of the hogtied lamb.
My childhood of sheep herding
with my dad came back

to me as Tom and
I squatted there taking pains
to disentangle

the little fellow
and set him free. The other
sheep had already

exited the yard
and returned to their pasture.
The lamb followed suit.

Houses Made of Stone

houses made of stone
and sinew and bone
give over to the morning

let go of bitter scorning
give thanks in your bed
rest your heavy head

Sun Behind Mountains

for Teigan Greenside

sun behind mountains
beginning to rise
on some unseen horizon

there are trees to get around
rough places to make
peace with this morning

Bad Blood

after Taylor Swift, for Renyel & Erik Shelton

We used to know how from what,
We used to know where we were going,
Till you pulled out the knife to cut

The rope that held the doorknob shut
To the basement where we were stowing
The pain of how, the lies of what.

And worse than that, you didn't let
The light shine where you were showing
The knife you planned to use to cut.

No wavering *if*, no plaintive *but*,
Just the blade suddenly glowing,
Cutting through to *how* from *what*

And now bad blood from heart to gut
The years I thought would keep on flowing,
Not this knife, this blood, this cut,

Not these problems in a rut
Where bad blood drowns love's knowing
Every inch of how and what,
How sharp the knife, how deep the cut.

The Sky This Morning

the sky this morning
had a moment of
pearl-like possibility
that then gave way to the gray
of a long gray day
closing like a shell

24.

復

Something Like the Sunrise

for Mark Shea

There was a time I thought the sun a dreary
Thing baring its teeth at my broken heart
Day after day to make me pay for the history
Of crimes I knew nothing of and thought my part
Inconsequential. I thought I needed saving
And that I must apologize every moment
For my existence and the inward raving
I offered to myself as a running comment
On absenteeism's unavoidable shame,
The insecurity of the crumbling ground
Beneath my feet. But then I knew the game
Was also something strange that could abound
In something like the sunrise in its beauty
That had no part of sorrow, shame, or duty.

This Morning Was a Long Time Ago

This morning was a long time ago,
a long time before the angels sent
a message from the river about the rent
after I'd gone back inside to go
to work to try to earn something to show
for all the alley shadows I was lent
and all the shades of charcoal black that blent
together in the moonset afterglow.

This morning was another world apart—
from where I am—when the sun began to rise.
Back then I was someone else in your eyes
and where I am was somewhere in my heart.
But this morning, long ago, I began to start
to see my way into the future of the sky.

The Sun Came Out

As if to vindicate the groundhog lore,
The sun came out on February 3rd.
I looked for it and stepped outside my door
To find it rising like a welcome word
That had been scarcely whispered the day before
But now was spoken clearly from the shore
Of the river where I often make absurd
Early morning visits like a bird.
The sun continued creeping through a cloud
Beyond the neighbors' house and up the sky.
The neighbors' tree let out a silent cry
Of glee and cast its shadow wide and proud
Across my feet where yesterday I plowed
The snow away with many a breathing sigh.

My Inner Rehab Project
for Nathaniel Lash

The sleep I had last night was like a hammer
Resounding in my inner rehab project
And when I woke this morning in the slammer
Of scattered thoughts and broken dreams, the object
Of love's laborious vision sharpened to
The sunrise in my eastward window pressing
Its face to smile abstractedly with blue
Arrays of hopeful songs and words confessing
Like a Beatles tune I'd never heard
Within my inner ear's admission of
A helpless abject poverty, a bird
That visits when you think there is no love
Left in the world but then you see the rising
Of day and sky unlocking and surprising.

Southbound Train
for Thomas Rist

southbound freight train crossing the river
for several days the sun's not been seen
i thought this morning would be the same
but the bruises in the sky began
to gather into a sunrise scene
and the feeling of being battered
began to feel like being alive
till the sun blasted through these thick clouds
like a southbound train with singing wheels

Feverish Sky
for Gabrielle Westcott

feverish sky on
the icy river
at the cusp of christmastide

and the beginning of the
return journey of
the warmhearted sun

Farewell Song to Summer

for Janice & Carroll Hayden

How many times have I stood
Beside this canal at the end of summer
In the early morning light
As the cool of autumn begins to sing?

How many songs does the earth sing
As petals fall where flowers stood
Season after season in changing light,
Autumn, winter, spring, summer?

How does autumn harmonize with summer
As both begin to strum and sing
The waves and particles of light
Where in the beginning God stood?

How has the universe withstood
The strangeness of the death of summer,
Year after year the dimming light,
The song no one seems to know how to sing?

And yet I sing where I have stood,
This half-light farewell song to summer.

Dream of Sleep-Driving

I'm at something like
a sleep disorder research
center, lying in

bed. An older gent
is standing there. (The doctor,
presumably.) He's

an upbeat, cheerful
fellow—reminds me of the
employment consultant

I worked with recently
on a job search, who in turn
reminds me of

Agent Lundy on
the TV show *Dexter*. He's
holding some vinyl

records, and one is
playing in the room—meant to
help me fall asleep,

I guess. (This echoes
a scenario in an
episode of the

TV show *Northern
Exposure* that my wife and
I watched recently,

where Dr. Fleischman
observes Maurice sleeping in
order to determine

whether he has sleep
apnea.) The music is
instrumental—

solo guitar of
some kind that reminds me of
a vinyl album

I owned back in the
days of vinyl albums:
Baroque Guitar.

"This reminds me of
baroque guitar," I say. I
fall asleep. When I

wake up, I discover
I've left the sleep center.
Presumably while

still asleep, I've driven
my car (which is a '65
T-Bird, the first car

I drove as a teen,
which is long since gone in real life)
to my eldest daughter's

apartment complex
to help her with some car trouble
she's having. I'm slightly

alarmed to have driven
while asleep, but relieved that
I don't seem to have

crashed into anything.
Sitting in the driver's seat,
I look around the parking

lot and spot my daughter's
car. I maneuver around
the lot and pull up

near her car. When I
get there, I find my younger
daughter kneeling down

beside her sister's
car. I see that she's trying
to blow air into

the tire, like you would
blow up a balloon. I think
to myself that this

probably isn't
going to work. In fact,
however, I then

observe that the tire
actually does appear
to be inflating.

The Duality

the duality
and imprecision
of all of reality
is as if the nothingness
has kissed the something
we are all missing

25.

無妄

Do You Know What It Means

I wake up in our hotel room
from a mint julep sleep
and wander down Canal
just as the sun burns through
the praline glaze of the sky
and makes the Mississippi shimmer.

I am like a man harnessed
to a plow, dragging it
towards the bright feeling
of a poem coming on,
and I am determined to
collaborate with the rising sun

to sow my iambic seeds
and let them grow with weeds
in minds now reading these
lines in places far away
from New Orleans' sugar fields
with no concern for harvests or yields.

A couple hours from now
my beloved and I
will board a plane and fly
back to the winter and dread—
and we will learn what it means
to miss New Orleans, like Louis said.

Innocence

for Mokeph Wildflower

Unintended innocence
meets the sky's quiet dissonance
as the sun skates through the layers
of winter's gray icy glaze
to make itself known in the
dormant melody of spring.

Le siffleux whistles a tune
stolen from the sun by the moon
that makes the shadows faintly dance
foretelling further darkness
in the realms beneath the ice
where the dawn still fails to break.

Le castor has secret ways
to carry the light in and out
among the fallen trees of doubt
until the shadows whisper
spring has come, the earth's reborn,
vigils has turned to matins.

And so the river of sky
continues its innocent flow
towards the ocean of heaven
where the blades of graceful skates
cut their arcs across the clouds
till the sun comes crashing through.

Our New Agenda

To test the limits of extreme bliss
We cancelled yesterday's agenda
And set our sights on a distant star.
But soon we found ourselves lost

Among pieces of space junk lost
In ill-conceived past missions of bliss,
Shards of rocketships with no agenda,
Flags that seemed to be missing a star

Or schoolchildren hoping for a gold star
But only feeling dashed and lost
When the teacher's stern agenda—
Red-ink slashes—trampled bliss

And left them seeking other bliss
Like an elusive Hollywood star
Stepped on without a plan or agenda
On the boulevard of the lost.

Now our bliss has a new agenda:
To find our star by being lost.

Sunrise in the Morning Mist

for Francis Waters

Sunrise in the morning mist
Reminds me that there does exist
A world beyond within my grasp
That slips away when I insist

On seizing it with forceful clasp
Or keeping it with lock and hasp,
But if I gently stand and look,
Breathe in the air without a gasp,

Give back the time that I once took,
Surrender king and queen and rook,
Let go my hold, unclench my fist,
The world will open like a book.

Common Loons

for Elizabeth Hart

common loons
are most uncommon
in my view

if you are
lucky you will see
and hear one

while you live
if you haven't yet
I advise

go to where
they dwell and wait there
till nighttime

be silent
and soon you will hear
the loon's wail

I Don't Exist
for Kevin Selby

back in kennewick i rise again
and make my way down to the river.
a few ducks and geese are gathered here,
oblivious to my arrival.
no one else around, i climb up on
a concrete block beside the shoreline
and stand here like a statue of man
left here after the apocalypse.
i don't exist but still see and love.

High Beams in the Rain
for Gloria Horton-Young

high beams in the rain
the driver intent
on getting somewhere as soon

as possible i stop time
climb in next to him
and write this poem

The Sunrise and I
for Tod Marshall

the sunrise and i
arrived together
by mutual agreement
at our old appointed place
like a prisoner
and a visitor

26.

大畜

Manuscript

for Kate Lebo

My manuscript of the morning light
waiting to be assembled
will draw upon reflections
that dance on the flowing
of this canal in spring.
The great poets will guide me.

The Path Forward
for Jack Webb

The path forward at day's dawn
suddenly reveals itself
to be the same path the greats
traveled. So call upon them now
to guide and help you on your way
through the brambles of beauty.

My Vision Is Set Ablaze

My vision is set ablaze
In breezes from poets I love
A tenuous flame that catches
This page of my poetry
To reveal hidden mountains
As hope disperses the clouds

As hope disperses the clouds
To reveal hidden mountains
This page of my poetry
A tenuous flame that catches
In breezes from poets I love
My vision is set ablaze

A Triolet from Memory

for Isaac Grambo

A triolet from memory
With rhymes and rhythms that recall
Its humble actuality:
A triolet from memory
Is like a choreography
Of stockings sliding down a hall:
A triolet from memory
With rhymes and rhythms that recall ...
And now you must repeat it all.

Like Water and Light

for Marilyn Sparks (in memoriam)

The cars on the highway stream
Like water and light in the old canal,
Like the memories of an old pal,
Like an escaping image from a dream.

Memories aren't always what they seem.
Recollections of some old gal—
Of cars in the highway stream
And water and light in the old canal—

Drinking coffee without cream—
Are not what is and ever shall
Be without end. My name's not Al.
It'll come to you in a brilliant beam
As cars on the highway stream
Like water and light on the old canal.

Recalling Times I Never Knew

Recalling times I never knew,
I woke this morning with the dew
And stepped outside to watch the sheaves
Of sunlight dancing in the leaves
Reminding me of me and you.

Two months ago when we drove through
Montana we knew what to do
To feel the magic up our sleeves,
Recalling times.

With summer days now slim and few
We wait to take off our last shoe
And meet again among the weaves
Where hide-and-seeking undeceives
The sunrise in eternal now,
Recalling times.

The Mind of William Butler Yeats
for Brian Waters

When I was standing at the garden gates
At sunrise on a Monday morning bright
Pondering the mind of William Butler Yeats,

It came to me that all the loves and hates
I'd harbored in the gyroscopic night
As I was standing at these garden gates

Were mostly matters best left to the fates,
Things I should have taken in my stride
Transposed against the mind of William Yeats.

Like melting runoff sifting through the grates
Of streets in ugly springtime's gross delight
So far from where I stand at the garden gates

As winter has its way with changing dates
And autumn puts up very little fight,
I think of the mind of William Butler Yeats,

The chaos and the beauty it creates
Within my own intention to abide
My own self standing at the garden gates
Pondering the mind of William Butler Yeats.

Streets Are Sheets of Ice

for Sam Waters

streets are sheets of ice
but the river holds
its own against the freezing

and speaks the faint hint of pink
from the sunless sky
like an unknown word

Anecdote of the Stats
for X. P. Callahan

My Substack stats
Are something that's
Been bugging me
Like walls with rats
Or chairs with cats.

They're on the rise
But I surmise
A lukewarm love
From Substack spies
With furtive eyes.

So I keep writing,
Sometimes citing
Things in Notes
I find exciting
And inviting

The Substack gods
To reck their rods
To read my poems
To stack the odds.
And then one hand applauds.

Where You Are Flying

where you are flying
to depends on your
individual mojo
arising from the choices
you have heretofore
made in this strange life

27.

頤

The Feasts of Others

Do not envy the feasts of others
imagined in the golden dawn
nor break your fast on fear.

Be the hungry tiger
or the self-sufficient turtle
nourished by goodness and light.

This Canal Is a Poet

for Frank (in memoriam)

This canal is a poet
Drawing from a river of words
And the tears of the mountains to
Irrigate the thoughts
And feed the feelings of the land
Under the eye of the sun.

This canal is a humble
Servant of the waters of life
Flowing down from the Cascade Range;
This canal bears the sun
Down from the frozen upper slopes,
Each molecule a syllable,

Each syllable forming on
The lips of the poet singing,
Continually melding and
Unmelding within the
Confluent intermingling
Of signifier and thing.

When I look at this canal
And consider its history,
Its beginning and end beyond
My experiencing,
I recall stepping into it
Once long ago and climbing

Back out, mortified and wet
But glad to have rescued a dog
Who wanted to run away and
Didn't see what he was
Getting into, a flow that would
Have carried him to heaven.

So, I return to my theme:
This canal is a poet and
I am that poet; this canal
And I are the same one,
And you, dear reader, are that dog,
Not biting the hand that feeds.

A Psalm
for Katherine Brown

When, ah, the Lord of Life beside me stands
down this deserted death I'm standing in
and lifts me, sifting sin like sand in His hands,
up to where the desert meets the green grasslands,
then my breaths are songs; nor can death win
when, ah, the Lord of Life beside me stands.

A pebble buried under shifting sands:
I am like entombed; my Lord calms the din
and lifts me, sifting sin like sand in His hands.

Hard pride Mine is crushed to dust by His commands:
crushed, emptied: humble temple of bones and skin
when, ah, the Lord of Life beside me stands.
Ah! How am I to answer death's demands
Save that my Lord reaches down, Across, Akin
and lifts me, sifting sin like sand in His hands?

He hangs my humility on supple strands;
I pray Not fall prey not fall in tangled spin
when, ah, the Lord of Life beside me stands
and lifts me, sifting sin like sand in His hands.

The Bare Ruined Limbs
for Alana Muir

the bare ruined limbs
of these trees contain
hidden rivers of the sun

where shadows not yet begun
feed the dreams of birds
and their silent songs

New Orleans
dozzina

The New Orleans I know is down in the delta
Where the Mississippi snakes its way in mud,
And telephone poles are slowly tipping over.
You see them from your train traveling south
From Chicago where you had a lucky layover
For a day at the Art Institute, looking at
American Gothic before climbing back
Aboard the train Goodman wrote a song
About and Arlo recorded for a beer,
The same train Binx and Kate took north
When flesh poor flesh was called upon to be
The end all and be all but quailed and failed.

I read the book and rode the train but failed
To reconcile what I knew about the delta
With the swamps I saw spread out like beer
Spilled across a tavern table to be
A sodden gateway to points further south,
The rails raised above the marshlands' back
Like a spine with tailbone through the mud.
And on my Walkman I listened to that song
As well as the young Bob Dylan's turnover
Of "shun that house in New Orleans" north
Of the Gulf of Mexico but south of desire at
My ten-dollar-a-night Orleans Hotel layover,

An upgrade from my first night's layover—
At the Le Dale, with rooms that failed
To provide a weary traveler much rest at
Night, cigarette smoke inhaling under south
Facing doors and bed-induced aching back.
What was it Percy said about the delta
Factor? Helen Keller naming mud
From water, lovely water, pouring over
Her hand as her teacher from the north
Spelled it in her other hand. Like beer,
The water took on what could only be
Felt as resplendent like a sudden song.

That was how, as if walking into a song,
I felt rising in New Orleans from a layover
Of twenty years before I bought a hardback
Edition of *The Moviegoer* while browsing at
Percy's favorite bookshop a little south
Of East Carrollton where I could've failed
Out of Tulane, enrolling from the north,
A reversal of Will Barrett in the mental mud
Of Central Park seeing a falcon over
The city with a telescope before he could be
Seen. But riding the streetcar was my delta,
Reading about Kate as I thought about beer,

Cape jasmine in Kate's lap, Dixie beer
And jambalaya on my mind, a jazz song
With trombone wafting up from Bourbon at
Saint Peter, near where the river turns north
In its twisting and turning to its own delta
Where dreams and gators rise from the mud.
Now three decades later I sit in the back
Of the same green streetcar heading south-
Southwest, then west-northwest over
To where I'll discover the now-failed
Ruins of Maple Street Books on a layover
In Audubon Park where a person can be

A person among birds and not have to be
Anyone in particular. To be such a be-er
In the heavy Louisiana air at
Two o'clock in the afternoon, the north
Forgotten and the strangeness of the south
Rife with signposts leaning over in the mud
Taking center stage and hearkening back
To that Randy Newman song, another delta
Between perception and reality when failed
Dreams are resurrected in a piano song
And a pleasant "Dixie Flyer" layover.
I could listen to that album over and over

And I did, when it came out, over
A year before I dreamt I could be
"Yes-sir-ree, in the land of reverie" back
When I also listened to Harry's song
About Basin Street. It also never failed
To combine, like a semiotic delta,
Multiple triangles of meaning writ in mud,
As I interrupted my education in the north
And took a leave of absence for a layover
In a train car traveling seemingly at
The speed of the sipping of a beer
In a dining car on the great plains, then south

To New Orleans, then east, and then south
Again to Florida to see Ron, then back over
The entire span of the country with a beer
For each day I was stuck on board and at
The mercy of the weather for a layover
Somewhere in the malaise of the north,
Feeling inwardly trapped, reading "The Delta
Factor" and Tolkien, reaching the back
Cover of the last book and its vision of failed
Humanity, not quite paradise regained, to be
Back in the shire with not quite a song
In my heart but something more like mud.

So here I stand in a spot where the mud
Of Audubon Park is the soil of the south.
A baker's dozen times—not just a layover
Along the Gulf coast but a true delta
Between the alpha and omega of my over
And under achieving life, my love song
To myself playing hide and seek in my back
Pages—I've visited here from the north.
Beignets and po'boys with coffee and beer,
Sazeracs and Hurricanes on Bourbon to be
Followed by an hour where jazz has failed
To be commercialized out of existence at

Preservation Hall or along Decatur at
Cafe Du Monde— my first stop, the mud
Of the Mississippi mingling with beer
And crawfish and oysters and catfish over
The Crescent Connection sunrise song
And the chugging of a tugboat in the delta
Dawn on its way to Baton Rouge and back
Out into the Gulf of Not America for a layover
In the narcissistic inevitable second failed
Presidency of a con artist from south
Queens coming down for the Chiefs, to be
Their bad luck, and ours, from the north.

I'm back at home now in the frozen north
With my beloved, a Montrealer, at
The kitchen counter listening to a song
By Ella, her favorite, and Satch from south
Of Rampart Street, pouring whiskey over
Ice cubes to stir into sazeracs for our layover
In the February blizzard of home, no beer
Left in the fridge, and no regrets about failed
Diets and the big easy weight gain like mud
Heavy in the rain of spring. The Delta
Flight that corkscrewed to a landing to be
Lying there like a beetle stuck on its back

Won't be the airplane that takes us back,
But there will be another in its failed
Wake that will someday succeed at
Transporting us again on angelic wings over
The fertile fields and cities flowing with beer
Like Jean Baptiste LeMoyne deBienville to be
Emissaries of love without a layover.
There's so much I haven't said in this song
To New Orleans and Walker Percy's South.
Perhaps like him I'll write a novel in the mud
Of my deeper longings and set it in the north
Or a thousand more poems, each a delta.

For now the delta of my own mind's mud
Lies still but flies over thoughts of the south.
I recall departing, and my next layover at
A museum in D.C., back when a song
Could pay for a beer and train ride north
And like New Orleans I could be happily failed.

28.

大過

Gongoozling Along
for Jo Magner

Gongoozling along
Little Venice's canals,
I came upon a heron
loitering for its breakfast
in the grey overcast dawn.
The heron eyed me, then took flight.

There was the suggestion
of a sunrise behind the
broken blinds of the old sky.
I carried an umbrella.
My beloved lay sleeping
back at her father's cousin's house.

What are you doing here?
I asked myself as the need
for coffee began to press.
I returned and turned the key
in one lock and the other,
opened the door and found my way

to the quiet kitchen—
the household not yet risen—
discovered light switches and
a coffee maker with pods.
I fumbled with the device
until I bent it to my will.

The Roof Beam Is About to Fall
for Writer Pilgrim

The roof beam is about to fall,
the dam is about to burst,
the plane is about to stall.

Animals begin to call
their warnings—softly at first—
that the roof beam's going to fall,

that danger has begun to crawl
on its way to worse from worst.
And the plane's begun to stall

with the coming of the squall—
its arrival unrehearsed—
and the roof beam fated to fall.

Calamity seems to enthrall
the passengers that are cursed
as the plane begins to stall.

But winged beauty's all in all
as the floodgates quench our thirst
as the roof refuses to fall
as the pilot takes control.

The Collapse of Night

The lordly husk of a dead tree
a few houses down from mine
stands like a pillar holding
up the wreckage of the sky.
The collapse of night comes soon
And with it, clarity of heart.

My Fifty-Ninth Birthday

sixty chunks of ice
floating near the shore
one for each of my fifty-nine

years just now melting away
plus the sixtieth
one I'm standing on

St. Joseph's Crutches
for Sophie Webb

i wait for my flight
and watch the blood-red
crown of the sun form above

the island of montreal
saint joseph's crutches
cluttering my mind

Its Destiny
for Fred & Ellen Hanson

the mighty columbia
beginning to break its fall
into the great pacific
spreads out a carpet of mud,
turns its back to the rising
sun to face its destiny:
the ferocious rolling sea

29.

坎

Wherever My Father Went
for Theodore Potter (in memoriam)

The morning clouds came and went,
came and went, and the breezes pink
made mauve-gold dimples where green grass bent.

The night was empty for having spent
its last gold coin on a deep drink
of morning clouds where they went

across the ripples that lent
the surface of the river's ink
these mauve-gold dimples where green grass bent

like the glassy eyes of an old gent
staring out and starting to think
about clouds that came and went,

came and went into the tent
of the day that was on the brink
of mauve-gold dimples where green grass bent.

Wherever my father went,
I can only recall and blink,
it was where the morning clouds were sent,
where mauve-gold dimples and green grass bent.

Toward the Sea
for Peter & Alice Kane

The abysmal morning
carries me on a current
of dismay at abyss
within abyss, and yet
the river of friendship continues
to flow toward the Sea—

I must believe it does
and that these many changing
lines must point to a place
downstream past these eddies
of confusion and propaganda
to where the river turns

again to flow toward
the places I love, west past
Umatilla, The Dalles,
Hood River, Multnomah
Falls, the criss-cross bridges of Portland,
Astoria, the Sea—

to join with the sunset
and ride the roller-coaster
of dangerous water
over the bucking bar
of November and into the calm
but terrifying Sea.

The River Rover
after Hopkins

I spied this morning morning's magus, flow-
  state of sunlight's orphan, supple-sum-swum Gander, in his swimming
    Of the pouring blending deep below him swirling flow, and brimming
  Low there, how he sung in answer to the shriek of a strident crow
In his buoyancy! then on, on current go,
  Cross-cast the wide wake. My thoughts were humming
    As a velvet thorn wheels round on a rose-rise: the hull and chimming
Howl for a fowl,—the alert of, the mystery of the show!

Svelte slyness and calmness and strength, oh, stream, dream, down, there
  Angle! AND the water that glides from thee then, the infinite
Frames filmed humbler, more aqueous, O my savoir faire!

  No magic of it: róugh rów makes murk scum suet
Gleam, and orange-black mirrors of the air
  Splash, mash the sun and this strange wild planet.

Scraps

for Michele Hobart (in memoriam)

Words I don't remember saying
Come back to me on paper scraps
I'm always writing and mislaying.

Sometimes I think I see you swaying
Toward carefully constructed traps
Of words I don't remember saying.

Sometimes I wonder if you're paying
The checks for million-dollar maps
I'm always writing and mislaying.

Could it be that I am praying
Your love may fill my gaps
With words I don't remember saying?

Could it rather be I'm playing
Variations on the theme of *Taps*
I'm always writing and mislaying?

Your name is what I find dismaying
When it, too, starts to collapse
Like a word I don't remember saying.

It visits a thousand times without staying.
It leaves because it sees, perhaps,
I'm busy writing and mislaying
Words I won't remember saying.

The Figgate Burn

where the figgate burn
pours into the firth
the sunrise in the distance

burns a hole in the morning
casts a spell on me
as i wake to sleep

The Shooter

on the movie set
the gun was loaded with blanks
they rehearsed the scene

did the actor know
was it just one of his pranks
like a movie set

he picked up the gun
did the character give thanks
to rehearse the scene

a roughhewn cowboy
riding horseback spurred the flanks
near the movie set

the gun was pointed
the river flooded its banks
they rehearsed unseen

nothing could be done
to stop the shuddering shanks
on the movie set
they rehearsed the scene

There Is No Was
for John Desmond (in memoriam)

there is no was there
is no is there is
no will be because the sun

rises the sun rises the
sun rises and we
are not really there

Fishing for Truth

Fishing for truth out of anything false
who is myself: reeling blindly a lie
on my line—the bottom of this shallow lake ...
some thought stretches but nothing crawls nearer
and who goes limp because the line
                                        snaps, meaning
no meaning to me ... clamouring in slime,
empty of face and having no good worms
to stab onto no hook and no good terms
to grab onto no life ... eyes see hands feel time,
but whose eyes who drops and bends, leaning ...
delicate water—the man from my mirror
whispering something about give and take
and me beginning to wonder—why am I
not myself?—why myself is not something else.

30.

離

Clinging Like Fire
for Ursula Potter

When I was sick or frightened,
before I understood the world
that had given birth to me,
my mother rocked me gently
and let me cling like fire to her
even as my flames floated

upward in a dance of light
and the discovery of love.
When I began to question
with open eyes and new words
why the world was the way it was,
my mother hedged a little

and pulled down a volume of
the encyclopedia set
that sat on the highest shelf
and opened it to a page
that she and I read together
until sparks flew off the page

and, like Moses' burning bush,
lit up the room with no damage
to the book or to our hands.
"The light shines in the darkness,"
she said as we returned the book
to its proper place above.

Hanging Fire Like an Old Suit
for Mathew Snyder

Hanging fire like an old suit
in the closet of high heaven,
the sunrise takes its sweet time
blinding the eyes of morning
while breakfast's thoughts of lunch
get run over on the road.

The silhouettes of lampposts
line the highway, some surveilling
with mounted cameras the dawn
while paltry hopes and slim fears
compel the coming storms
to hasten from the ocean.

Meanwhile, up above, the blue
and the green of the ancient sky
convey a broad and serene truth
difficult to comprehend
but nonetheless present
in the escaping feeling

of aimless anxiety
beginning to fetch a glimpse of
the raw buoyancy of tires
on lined and mangled asphalt,
repaired and re-repaired
dozens of times in the sun.

Dark Glow

for Richard & Camille Potter

My father's guns, left to me—
Several from the bedroom closet
And one from under the bed:
Shotgun with a flashlight taped
To the barrel to daze the eyes
Of a midnight intruder.

The light my father wielded
He left to me in my midnight.
I unloaded the rifle
And held it in the sunrise.
The black barrel's golden gleaming
Gave off a dark glow of love.

The Sky at First Glance

The sky at first glance today
was like a cave painting
from a paleolithic
morning and I felt my sleep
had been cut short by its music
clinging to my heartbeat till I woke
and went outside to fathom
with my seven senses
the dimensions of the day.

I couldn't get away from
the intensity of that sky
even though for a moment I tried
and thought about returning
to my bed to fall back
to the sleep of my distant
tribal ancestors clinging
to their campfires as the flames cling
to the wood and as I cling to you.

The Burning Sky

The burning sky reminds me I'm in love
With you. As if I need reminding. I look
Up at the clouds and down the street where morning's
Shadows and glinting metals form a hallelujah
To the molten dawn, its orange and bitter beauty,
Its pools of gold and columns of light pointing
Me to where I'd like to be: with you
Beyond the eastern horizon, where the blue
Sky of day has advanced with ashes anointing
The weariness of planetary duty,
The in-between of flying over Montana,
Heeding the cautious captain's seatbelt warnings
While calmly watching a movie or reading a book;
To get to you, that's what I'm thinking of.

New Orleans Deluge

From the end of Canal Street, looking across
The river to Algiers and McDonogh and Whitney,
I ponder the sun's gain and loss,

And whether the weather will suddenly hit me
With sheets of rain and fists of wind
Like Monday evening when we rode in a jitney

Through flash-flooded streets where we grimly grinned
At the faces of folks who were fleeing for cover
Or wading through puddles, soaked or bare-skinned,

As thunder and lightning made good to deliver
More buckets and barrels and tubs of rains
From voodoo tricksters in the sky where they hover

Invisibly, risibly, dancing the pains
Away with the torrents flowing in streams
And spouting like fountains up from the drains

Until the night came down with its dreams,
A blanket of gray hiding the stars,
And a new moon with clouds shrouding its beams

Until Canal Street woke up and streetcars
Began to travel their ancient tracks
And workers began to clean the bars

Of Bourbon Street, the trash in sacks,
The sun not seen. But now, a day later,
The dawn is getting through these cracks

To smile like a grinning alligator
Or like a gold-toothed voodoo boss
Or a crazy sunrise poem creator.

Approach
for Keith Aron

Early morning flight path
descends to Montreal
as the sun's ascension
presses pink and orange
up against the wind wall
of the cold-sky river.

Flight attendants secure
the cabin for landing
as the bare limbs of night
prepare for the morning
and the winter begins
to succumb to the spring

sunrise vomiting love
in violent beauty
as the morning gives birth
in purple majesty
to the golden-splayed day
and the burden of light.

In solidarity
and relief, the music
of the river and sky
and the thawing of the
long-frozen ground combine
to make a dancing rise

up from the roots in time
for me to join despite
the windchill undeceiving
me of my urge to bare
my skin to the burning
of a molten skyline,

retreating to the car
to await the breaking
there next to the bridges
with the planet's turning,
the sun the sun the sun
burning with all its might.

Above a House
for Betsy Sivula

pre-raphaelite
pigments in the sky
shot out from the horizon

above a house and its trees
bruised blue electric
gold-vermillion sun

Mon Amour and I

mon amour and i
wait by the river
for the sun to deliver

its message of morning light
written in golden
lines on the water

Connective Tissue

for Benjamin & Mary Peterson

connective tissue
of the morning light
even when the sun's obscured

and the houses are inured
in their own malaise
soon come brighter days

31.

咸

Was I the Sun or the River

was i the sun or the river
and were you the bird or the branch
when we were drawn together

each ripple in the river
a wave and you and i take
turns being the crest and the trough

Sunrise Wooing

The sunrise woos me to wake up
just as my beloved woos me
to continue dreaming into day
while she rides the train of love
to endure her day of work,
wooing me silently

every breathing moment of
the workday she suffers through,
every twinge of her torn meniscus
continuing to hobble
her best intentions to run
after me in triumph.

What else can I tell you about
my bedazzled beloved one?
She inhibits her nimblest features
which nonetheless radiate
from her as from a goddess
seated above Athens.

Her tongue, usually hidden,
can speak like rose petals in spring
and acrobatically navigate
two mother tongues, the sunrise
and the sunset, while wooing
me continuously.

Superior Sunrise
for Kent Peterson

Having no sunrise of my own
I looked around and found
A red one with a purple tone uploaded by a fella's phone
Who lives in Wisconsin and is renowned
For manual typing
A daily missive
And rarely griping
About the elusive
Search for happiness at the end of one's fingers
Tapping keys
While the sunrise lingers
In early morning mysteries
On a porch he constructed like a ship
Facing the lake's pointing fingertip.

The Shade Is Pulled

The shade is pulled above our bed, and through
The silken hanging drapes the sun affixes
Its beam to cast our shadows on the blue,
The pale-blue, green-blue walls where color mixes
With a vibrant painting painted by your mother,
Of pink and white flowers in a vase
That seem to be finale of some other
Suspended history of time and place.
Imagine Wallace Stevens played by Bill
Murray and the emperor like a groundhog
Finding his way over a distant hill
For the first time after that repetitive slog
Of doing time in Plato's illusory cave,
Then waking up free, no longer a slave.

Sunset Sonnet

When I arrived, a man and woman standing
there were pointing at the shadows where
they saw a deer half-hidden in the trees.
I looked but couldn't see so smiled and carried
on with my run down the paved trail
along the river, listening to music, my ears
full of the sound, my eyes full of the sky,
so much so the birds and colors began to cry.

Earlier, in the garage, where I was clearing out
my father's things, I'd found a piece of paper,
some plans for a jewelry box he'd made for you.
And on the back, addressed, it seemed, to me:
"I hear you"—in his handwriting as if written
just then to let me know and feel and see.

Dog & Horse Dream

I'm back at Mom's and
There's a problem with dogs barking
in the backyard.

Apparently, she's
taking care of another
dog or two besides

Toby, and they're causing
a ruckus. I go out
to the yard and try

to restore order.
There's a horse there, too, and I
think that maybe if

I can get the horse
to lie down on the lawn and
take a nap, then the dogs

will follow suit and
calm down. I seem to be well
acquainted with the horse—

a sable mare—
and she cooperates
easily with me.

I lie down on the grass
and she follows my lead.
As she lies down

next to me, I take care
to avoid being crushed by her.
All's well.

Children

for Margaret Ann Silver

Some are desperately
trying to have them,
others are desperately
trying not to,
some will abandon them
when they do,
others sneak into hospitals
to steal them.

Then we send them
off to school,
we push them
onto buses and into classrooms,
send them to the
Island of the Young
where they form
tribes and alliances.

We usher them
here and there,
to soccer games
and birthday parties,
piano lessons and malls.
We don't know
what to make of them,
nor they us.
But we catch glimpses
of each other in the mirror.

Caricatures
of ourselves, we are
lost in a whirlpool
of DNA and love
and blunder.
And it is both shocking
and unsurprising
when they become us
as our stars gradually fade
in their beautiful dawn.

The Way

The way
the sky
plainly
spreads out
above
the plains
reminds
me of
the way
the thought
of you
my love
always
lingers
over
the plain
mundane
this and
that of
my days.

32.

恆

An Ordinary Day Begins
for Roger Scott

An ordinary day begins
With the smooth clarity of
The glow cast by intense
Burning under the soft clouds.
Let it burn the bad poetry
Of the past and write a new song

On the railroad cars of the day.
They're keeping still by moving,
Persisting into the light
Of a landscape scrolling by,
Singing a train song without words,
Against but with the river's flow.

The Continuity of Sky

for Yvonne Leach

The continuity of sky
Above the absurdities
Of the highway and constant
Pep rallies of artifice
Is there for us if we merely
Lift up our eyes to the heavens.

The Duration of the Sunrise
for Alan Shelton

The duration of the sunrise
Is continuous motion
Enduring to the end of
This sweet life as we know it.
But the end is the beginning,
And a new sun will always rise.

It Furthers

It furthers the sunrise to have
This fine rollercoaster of ripples
To carry its light forward
Towards my heart's intention
Now found in the day's duration
And the race to the finish line.

Another Year

Another year for you my dear
Time slips away but that's okay
The clock that ticks you need not fear
Just let it go, unseize the day
Enjoy the falling and the breeze
The turning planet and the sky
The flooding rivers and the seas
Then turn to face me eye to eye
To hear my words and songs of birds
That tell you things you always knew
Like time divided into thirds
Like you love me and I love you
The was, the will be, and the now
Are in your hand, you guide the plow

My Hometown Enduring

my hometown enduring
the sun making bold to rise
the empty canal ready

to resume its seasonal
flow past the calm of the backyard
my self grieving to be leaving

33.

遜

In Retreat from the Night
for Brad Green

in retreat from the night
every breath along the river
is held like a loaded gun

there's no need to press forward
take a step back and remain
hidden like the coyote

The One Moment

for Henry Koski (in memoriam)

All the times I've looked at this tree
With the sun coming up behind
Its branches signaling me
In a way aloof but kind,
I've felt something stir inside
My heart that I thought had died.

I've had to turn away, retreat
From the blinding light of that thought,
But even then the something sweet,
The something that can't be bought,
Has lingered, an aftertaste
Of something that can't be chased.

So I take a step back, exist
In the one moment that contains
Everything I somehow missed
In all my pleasures and pains,
And wait for some kind of sign
In the shadows soft and fine.

Montana
for Holland Potter

The hurly-burly hills of Montana
Remind me of a life I've never lived,
Some other life I might have had if I
Were someone else but still my selfsame self
Riding on horseback across this valley.

Our Lady of the Rockies scans the sky
From the Continental Divide to the
Beginning of the end of the union
And seems to nod to me as if to say,
You are not who you are in Montana.

Driving from Idaho through St. Regis,
Skirting Missoula, arriving in Butte,
I pull off the interstate and find myself
In the old uptown, laid out on a hillside,
Waiting for an unlikely renaissance.

Get out of there fast and continue on
To Bozeman where an academic glow
Elevates the general crud to something
That could make a case for surviving winter
To get some know-how and a few credits.

What am I doing in Montana?
I ask myself. There's almost no speed limit
Here, which doesn't make much difference because
The landscape swallows you up at any speed.
What I need is a horse to make my escape.

The Fog Again
for Robert Wrigley

The fog again has settled in
Along the river like a skin,
Beyond the bridge where thought ascends
The lengths of cables to their ends,
Stretched taut and hooked with bolt and pin.

Clark and Lewis and their men
Came this way, the west to win,
And later found that winter sends
The fog again.

Sacagawea and her kin
Saved them from their own chagrin
To find the river where it bends
Towards the ocean where it blends
With sunrise hidden there within
The fog again.

Aquamarine Jewel Sun

aquamarine jewel sun
rests amid a bed of dark clouds
i adjust my expectations

for the day and follow you
my beloved into love
balancing poetry and rest

Sunrise from the Rose

for Kristi & Bob Morgan

sunrise from the rose
garden this morning
a squirrel in a nearby tree

chattering at me it seems
summer dwindling
down all around me

The Outskirts of Town at Dawn

I found myself on the outskirts of town at dawn
And wondered how I'd ended up awake
To see the rising of the devil's sun.

I stepped out into the wind and thought I'd run
But then I took a breath and tried to shake
Myself awake on the outskirts of town at dawn.

The wires in the sky seemed to hum a tune
That mixed inside my head and seemed to break
Like waves arising with the devil's sun.

And then your call came ringing like a gun.
I wondered if it was you or just some fake
Imposter of myself on the outskirts of town.

Should I answer or should I throw my phone
Into the fire of the burning lake
To answer to the devil's risen sun?

I answer and I hear your voice alone
Telling me to come home for goodness' sake,
To bring myself from the outskirts of the town
And leave the devil and the rising sun.

Substack Haiku Sequence
for Bashō

1.
In the dark, the light
Of my phone's screen casts shadows
Across my wife's face.

2.
Give them a platform
To stand on, and they will show
You how they can dance.

3.
Substack is to X
As New Orleans is to Hell
As poetry is.

4.
There are poets here
But these Procrustean screens
Cause their lines to wrap.

5.
James Joyce could be here
Gradually amassing
His pomes penyeach.

6.
Bashō writes haiku
And posts them to a Substack
Made of butterflies.

7.
Sign up for a free
Or paid subscription as they
Migrate into sleep.

I Recall What I Forget
for Peter Blasevick

as the sun begins
its southward retreat
due to the tilt of the earth

i recall what i forget
and grasp at passing
thoughts passing away

Ragged Ridges

for Jeanne Murray Walker

the mountains surround
bozeman like cupped hands
the sunrise comes late over

ragged ridges' majesty
catching hold of wires
strung with pearls of light

The Oratory

the oratory
with all its crutches
is there on the horizon

a wall of clouds behind it
and the sun climbing
up that wall for me

34.

大
壯

I Woke in a Fit of Dark Unease
for Brooke Matson

I woke in a fit of dark unease
with an ache of anger and ego
putting out my inner light
in the middle of a strange
and feverish autumnal night,
and willed myself to stay awake.

My waking surged weirdly in my soul
to separate my self from my wrath
and muster up a vigor
for the coming of the day
and the challenges of my dread
deep in my chest and in my head.

I then made my way to the river
and the river made its way to me,
eddying and undulating
at my feet, hesitating
to pull away the curtain of sky
to reveal a cautionary

and encouraging tale of changing
lines and blooming fanfare in the clouds
as well as inside of me,
we being one and the same,
as shadows began to settle
and the day in fine fettle dawned.

My First Step

for Ann Dyer & James Hiers

The point of this exercise
is to walk the stepping stones
of gold light from the sunrise,
to let gold infuse one's bones
with faith to walk on shards of light
without submerging back to night.

The sun has crept up behind
a wall of cloud to convey
an eye peeking through a blind,
a line of sight to belay
the boat that might today set sail
to take me where it cannot fail.

So I imagine taking
my first step like Saint Peter
or like a toddler making
a move to walk and teeter
toward the thrill of waking words
and a murmuration of birds.

So the sunrise charts my path
and the oracle of days
frees me from the risk of wrath,
assures me of breezy ways
singing my sails towards the sea
to a new world awaiting me.

Love Is Strong
for Art & Cheryl Klym

I followed the morning down
to where the river flows by
gently but powerfully
carrying future thunder
like a deliberative judge,
like a jury with a verdict
waiting to be delivered,
waiting to crash forth across
the bar into the Pacific.

A spray-painted "Love is strong"
on a concrete block the message
the morning wants to tell me now
as the news from upstream floats
slowly down from the mountains,
as my blood flows through my veins,
as the power of outrage
builds in the broken pieces of
what is left of justice and love.

Bang! Bang! the Drum!

for Romeo Mendoza

Bang! Bang! the drum!
With wooden sticks
And hands fisted,
Bappety-bop, bappety-bop
And a bing-bong and a ding-dang
Mister Harry!
My friend Larry
On the bass
To play a song—
Come dance with us!

Travis Laurence Naught

Your body's lack may have been ever
So furthering but you prevail
By daily grit to push the lever—
Propels the roulette wheel to sail
Your chair's unsisyphean rolling
Down sidewalks like a cop patrolling
The beat for poets on the loose,
Some wild and caffeinated goose,
To conquer fear itself by sporting
Anxiety's undouble down
With help from town to town to town
With lustful thoughts cavorting courting
Love's trailing tall tales on the wheels
Of what a journaled virgin feels.

Karen Mobley

I see your face through tears unburdened
From underneath the deep blue sky
Where Gold Beach mother's smooth ungardened
Implicit agates seem to cry
For fishing poles unheld by father
And sun signs synchronized with brother,
Ordeals and trials, despair a toy
With which we seem to wrestle joy.
Your one wing melted, still the other
Persists to make the art we see,
To make who see believe and be
What we would be by our own druther
Because God gave us fantasy
And eggs and apples crisp and free.

Chris Cook

Others erstwhile called you Cookie—
Perhaps due to your cagey way
Of showing normal life is tricky
With colors dancing in the gray
And hidden in the shadows furtive
Fables awaiting light from votive
Candles imparting the glow of grace
On animalia's inner-space
And humankind's unlikely pairing
Of metaphoric trumpet blasts
With Fred and Ted tied fast to masts
Of childhood's daring and uncaring
While Cookie beats the sirens' rhyme
Into a damn good broken time.

Nance Van Winckel

But I shrug off the broken weather
Of these, these awful times, while Nance—
The light of her, as from another,
A better, world—creates a trance
Of poetry and sanity to
Improve our luck by looking down—too
Awake to let us lose this chance
To be less busy and to dance
Down Zupeck Street with broken stroller,
Angelic hawk's unlikely flight
Into the silver thread of night
To reach that mole like a lost dollar
That little girl perhaps could see
But couldn't reach to shake it free.

35.

晋

I Dreamt of My Father Last Night
for Roger Potter

I dreamt of my father last night
on the anniversary eve
of his death three years past.
Things were easy in the dream—
despite his brother's flat tire and
dilapidated trailer.

When I woke it was still dark out
and my travel day lay ahead.
The sun rose easily
and easiness continued
until I had boarded my flight—
three exit-row seats all mine.

Now I find myself in the air
watching a movie about grief
with gorgeous scenery—
my progress easy like that,
my grief a bit of bumpy air,
my father's love a smooth flight.

This Morning's Waking

for Randal & Michelle Potter

This morning's waking came down like an anvil
my father's elbow nudged by accident
in heaven's workshop where it tumbled
through the clouds and sunrise filament
and landed with a thud, abrupt but gentle.
Awakened from the darkened firmament
of deepest sleep, I stood and turned the handle
to open wide the door with mild excitement.
The sunrise drivers on the highway glistened
beneath the ordinary glory of the sky,
their right feet on the pedals as they hastened
to Tuesday obligations, tired and chastened,
with thoughts of Thursday's coming pumpkin pie—
the third Thanksgiving since my father died.

The Moon That Rose
for Bliss Grey

The moon that rose
Last night was like another night.
The moon that rose
That other night without its clothes
Of clouds was like this moon a sight
That made my heart tug like a kite
The moon that rose.

Escape

Escape with me, my love, on metal wings
And let us flee this icy island, south
To where the sun has fled with all good things,

A game of hide and seek that winter brings —
So let us seek the hiding place of warmth:
Escape with me, my love, on metal wings.

Let us go to where some mermaid sings
About the sunrise and what lies beneath
The place the sun has fled with all good things.

Let's leave this ice-bound river's lovely stings
And fly the sky-path to escape the wrath
Of winter, yes, escape on de-iced wings.

Let's be like grapes some slingshot flings
Into a smiling goddess's magical mouth
Down where the sun has fled with all good things

To be consumed and born again with rings
Of flowers round our suntanned bellies' girth.
Escape with me, my love, on metal wings
To where the sun has fled with all good things.

The Remedy
for Armin & Beth Vogt

The sunrise on the Selkirks, through the trees
Of my old street recovered from the past,
Becomes a remedy for my disease.

I'm standing here, not falling to my knees.
I only stand as witness to what's cast
The sunrise on the Selkirks through the trees.

The future's in my pocket, if you please.
Perhaps it's just the breaking of my fast
Becomes the remedy for my disease.

I have three dice and all three come up threes,
Pointing to the present that's at last
The sunrise on the Selkirks through the trees.

The moment sneaks up on me like a sneeze
That makes me cough and shudder from the blast,
A sudden remedy for my disease.

The morning carries on into the breeze.
I can't recall why I felt so aghast.
The sunrise on the Selkirks through the trees
Becomes the remedy for my disease.

Thirteen Ways of Looking at the Sunrise
after Stevens

I
There is no sun,
There is no rise.
There is only the poet, watching.

II
When I arrived at the river
There were only these three geese
Secreting three sunrises.

III
The sunrise shattered like stained glass.
It was a slow-motion moment soon past.

IV
The river and the mountains
Are one.
The river and the mountains and the sunrise
Are one.

V
I am guilty of
Counting syllables
When confronted with the sun
About to rise or having
Risen as I stand
There in the silence.

VI
As winter comes on,
The sun rises further and further
Away on the despondent horizon.
The poet's entrepôt of words
Grows fogbound
With the temptation of silence.

VII
O sleeping people of Umatilla,
Why do you suppose the sunset
Will suffice for beauty?
The Columbia flows east for
Only a short while
Before it turns to bring you the sunrise.

VIII
I have been to London,
Paris, Vienna, Edinburgh, Galveston,
New Orleans, Montreal, and Seattle,
And have seen the same sunrise,
Or seemingly the same,
As in these channeled scablands.

IX
When the sun began to rise,
It made the horizon
One of many horizons.

X
At the sight of the sunrise
Splurged as if from the cannula of a mad painter,
Even the stags of scarcity
Would pause and look up.

XI
She stood at the kitchen window
And stared out at the November gloom,
Fearing for a moment that
The headlights on the highway
Were the remnants of last year's sunrises.

XII
The moon is setting.
The sun must be rising.

XIII
It was sunset all afternoon.
It was raining
And it was going to rain.
The sunrise remained
In the poet's limbs.

The Sunrise on the Land Beyond
for Ann Collins

The sunrise on the land beyond
The river flowing to the sea
Calls to mind the day that dawned,
The sunrise on the land beyond,
Before the dams when salmon spawned,
No gate, no border, lock or key,
The sunrise on the land beyond
The river flowing to the sea.

The End of the Road
for Joseph Reiss

the end of the road
is where the sunrise
begins to become the day
ambling nonchalantly
towards you with a
slow but steady grace

36.

明夷

Like the Invisible Sun

for Odo Recker, OSB

Like the invisible sun
in its own semi-secret blue
sky behind the seven veils
of the hundred clouds of morning,
I find myself inwardly rise
to my unspoken occasion.

In the Light of the Sun's Rising
for John Liem

The moon in the light of the sun's rising
Presides above the falling world
Where all and nothing is surprising
To people flying as if hurled
By the unseen hand of a sinker pitcher
And death itself the absent catcher
Beyond horizons in the end
Waiting like a friendless friend
Who takes your hand and smiles grimly
As the sun begins to set
As if pierced by bayonet,
The blood red sky then fading dimly
Into darkness with its stars
And sleep to numb autumnal scars.

Road Kill
for Jeff Marty

It was Saturday morning, the end of September, and I
Had my hands on the wheel and my mind on the words that I felt
Coming at me: coyote and carrion crows. And the sky
After sunrise had shone its great light on the blood and the pelt
Of some creature who'd met with some car on that long stretch of road.
The coyote inspecting, bewildered, looked over at me
As I made my approach as a human transmitting my code
And attempting to fathom the scene and assess could it be …
Were the bones and the fur and the blood that was spilled
The remains of a second coyote? The blood was so vast
On that road where this creature was run down — I wondered who'd killed
It, what human with what kind of shadowy future and past
Zeroed in, a trajectory, savagery, metal and bone
And the way of the world when you drive through it lost and alone.

My Poetry
for Eric & Anne Spencer

Holding onto this hope
In inevitable failure
I surrender my own ego
As I contemplate my skill
Darkening into night
The force of fire lingers here

The Smoke from Fires All Around Us
for Silvia Kalina

The smoke from fires all around us
Obscured the sun whose fire burned
Anemically till morning found us
Accepting what we hadn't learned
Till eating breakfast and recalling
Those warnings that we found so galling
From Gilbert Plass and later Gore
And ever since then many more
With assholes in the halls of Congress
Unleashing idiotic dogs
To piss on the scientific logs
And question scientists' consensus
That we are up a smoldering creek
With burning paddle—and it's bleak.

Dream of the Doctor and the Mask

I'm accompanying someone—
possibly my mother but also
possibly my father.

Or it could be some other
loved one. It's not clear
in the dream. But I'm

standing there
as a concerned person.
We are in the office area

of a clinic or hospital,
in a cubicle
with a desk and computer.

My loved one is sitting there
in close proximity to the doctor
who is sitting at his computer

looking at an image or lab results
or something
on his monitor.

I'm standing, hovering
over them because
the space is small

and there's no place to sit.
There's a grim feeling in the air.
The doctor is wearing scrubs

and a sort of ugly blue flannel mask
that he pulls away from his mouth
when he speaks.

I'm astonished that
(a) he's wearing a cloth mask
and not a medical grade one

and (b) he keeps pulling it
away from his face when he talks
in such close proximity

to my loved one (and now
I think it is my mom).
I start to say something,

to complain or question,
but my mom interrupts
and points out the issue with the mask

herself. The doctor acts defensive
and mumbles something
about masks being ineffective.

But he adjusts it
so it covers his face properly
and continues.

Courtside

Celebrities attending sporting events
Intermingling with the wives of players
Oblivious to the riots going on
Appear on screen following dramatic plays
And we forget about the children starving,
Imagining sitting there courtside with them.

37.

家人

Each Person Is a Genius
for David Garrigues

Each person is a genius—
extruded from the collective
unconscious, the family
of things and non-things burgeoning
into the light of morning,
the lovely light of the dawn.

Imagine a boat anchored
through the night now awakening
with a family on board
ready to break their fast and hoist
their sails, each member playing
a part in the yin and yang

of the embarkment into
the final joys of the summer
tapering down to its end,
the current and wind ready to
take them towards the ocean,
towards the glowing horizon.

And beyond that, day and night
proceeding towards the autumn,
the falling leaves and harvest
brought in and shipped to distant ports,
infinitely distant ports
yet each infinitely near.

Electric Lightbulb Standing in for the Sun

Electric lightbulb standing in for the sun
On Rue Drummond in Montreal. It's snowing
But the snowflakes become raindrops again as they
Melt against my face and the pavement. I'm walking
To a cafe of warmth to climb inside and drink
A mug of cafe au lait while mon amour faces the day
On her own and soldiers on the way she must
Because because because because because
That's just the way it goes. Meanwhile my lust
For life and her simmers on the back burner
Of the electric stove of the autumn of our life
And the comforts of love's couch cushions,
Though grown a bit lumpy, nonetheless
Continue to bless, to bless, to bless, to bless.

Chicago
dozzina

The train ride Binx and Kate took
In *The Moviegoer* was my introduction
To the thought of Chicago before I ever
Visited that grand city as a stop
On my drive across the country in a car
With a starter that was going bad—
At every stop refusing to start,
Which caused me to take it to a shop
And strand myself there for three days,
Sleeping in the cargo hold.
(It was a Volkswagen Rabbit and I
Made myself a bed there.)

The mechanic, wheelchair bound, said there
Was a part he'd need to order, which took
A couple of days, which wasn't bad.
I grabbed my guitar by way of introduction
And rode the "L" downtown to start
Some kind of adventure: a donut shop
Where a girl said, "Do you only hold
That thing or can you play it?" So I
Pulled it out and played what I called "Used Car"
By Springsteen, and scored the day's
First donut and coffee and the first ever
Bit of fame I thought might never stop.

That lovely girl, though, was my last stop
On a slippery slope that started there
And ended up back at Dave's shop
In the malaise of the night and my bad
And solitary bed. On the third day, I
Rose from my parking lot tomb, as ever.
Dave finished the job and I paid seven days'
Of my budgeted cash to get the car
Out of there and on the road. I took
It about a mile and, to see if it'd start
Again, pulled off, cut the motor, took hold
Of the key again and suffered a reintroduction

Of the problem whose first introduction
Had occurred in Idaho on my first stop
Of the trip. Never mind. Cut to many days
And nights and years later. Chicago took
Its place as the halfway point where I
And thou would meet and put our lives on hold
To navigate the genie soul of wind whenever
We could, hand in hand without a car,
From O'Hare on separate flights to start
Our explorations of the good and bad —
Trump Tower evincing the latter there;
The former, the Art Institute and its gift shop.

In love, we roamed from shop to shop
And made an extended introduction
Of art and architecture, taking time to stop
For views and drinks to sip and hold
While gazing lovingly, thou and I,
Into each other's reveling to be there
With each other. Rarely, we'd hire a car
To get from point A to B with a bad
Driver at the wheel in a kind of daze
That made us wonder how many drugs he took.
Other times we'd rent bikes to start
A ride along the lake that could go forever.

Those were the days of after ever
After, when Chicago set the scene to shop
For the future of our new life and fresh start,
Looking at our reflection there
In the bean in Millennium Park, like a stop
On the rollercoaster of time, the bad
Interlude behind us and the days
Of boat rides through downtown and car
Rides in the countryside before us, I
With my daughters and you with your son. They took
To us graciously as the introduction
To this new life began to take hold.

In my Chicago mind, I hold
An image of us at Montrose Beach, wherever
The path had led us, an introduction
To Lake Michigan and a place to start
Our walk along the shore, the wind not bad,
The autumn sun like a golden car
Cruising up the sky while thou and I
Walked like angels ascending to a stop
For lunch at London House, the rooftop there
Commanding views of every café and shop,
And surrounding buildings that, when we later took
The river tour, would fill our minds for days.

That afternoon seemed to stretch for days
As we sat together on a boat built to hold
A hundred tourists or more sitting there
With us to see the Aqua with its ever
Undulating lines, Wrigley's eye
To terra cotta connecting good and bad,
Marina City's corncob look and onsite shop—
No need to leave or have a car.
We cruised along and gawked and took
A thousand pictures, our river-introduction
To amazements that seemed to stop
Time in its tracks, until we made it start.

Our Chicago times, from the very start,
Were some of our very best days,
Even when we got our introduction
To Pilsen, staying near the Pink Line stop,
Up the crookedest stairs we'd ever
Seen to an iffy AirBnB above a shop.
We bought a dozen eggs and I
Cooked them for every meal we ate there
Till we decided it was time to put a hold
On eggs—not that they were at all bad!—
And venture out for Mexican art that took
The cake and then to Cindy's in a car.

An elevator car, that is, a car
That took us to the rooftop for drinks to start
An episode of elegance and views from there
To the bean below and then a repeat introduction
To the Hampton Social, near a beauty shop
Not far from Navy Pier, our favorite ever,
Maybe, a place to put your cares on hold
And enjoy authentic refinement that puts a stop
To the threat of the malaise—not that you or I
Were in any danger, being so in love we took
Each other's breath away and all the days
Blurred into nights when nothing bad

At all could happen. Except for that one bad
Sandwich we ate that laid us low there
For but a blip, redeemed by Dogs for days
Found recommended with celery salt at the start
Of our third visit when we opted for an introduction
To the theatre district and the Kimpton Allegro. We'd stop
For champagne in the sparkling lobby and shop
For finery and memorabilia after we took
In *Bernhardt/Hamlet* at the Goodman. If ever
We'd had a glitzier time of lovely fun, we'd hold
That thought aside like a parked car
And just enjoy the loveliness of thou and I.

The next day, being librarians, you and I
Paid our respects to the public library with its bad-
Ass owls, then walked by Buckingham Fountain near there,
St. Peter's Church in the Loop, its rosary shop
And streetwise crucifix to make the traffic stop.
We were veritably floating from now to ever,
Wondering at our lovely luck and lucky start
And this recurring windy city introduction
To the strange turn we'd taken in our souls' car,
Traveling to the next opportunity to hold
Each other and to float in the air for magical days
On end and offer up whatever it took.

Back to O'Hare and its brachiosaurus, I took
My flight and you yours, to start our introduction
To a few weeks' separation. Not forever, not too bad,
Because we'd soon shop for flights to London and there
Eke out a weeklong stop before the pandemic took hold
Like a swerving car that changed the course of our days.

Jeanie Elizabeth

Jibbity-jabbity
Jeanie Elizabeth
Was my big sisterly
Guide to the light.

In the sweet seventies
Psychomagnetically
All through that decade we
Fought the good fight.

38.

瞵

Nine Dawns

I.
The sunrise can be
as shocking
as a murder scene
or as grizzly and beautiful
as a roadside accident
where much lifeblood has been spilled.

II.
The bones of the sky are soaked
in gasoline and orange rind
and set on fire.

III.
If you know the layout of the town
like a delivery driver knows it,
then you can look at its lights
from this hilltop
in the lightening morning
and spot Smith's angel on Gage Boulevard
and imagine the Starbucks nearby
and the smell of espresso.
And then allow yourself to take in the sky,
the shaft of faint yellow light
shooting up from the horizon
and the fronds of darkness
against an orange catastrophe
of unrequested beauty.

IV.
The three pavilions at the top of Hills West,
and the benches where no one sits,
overlook the Yakima's sad and lovely merger
with the Columbia in all its muscular calm.
Away from the southward trending of the sunrise
the pink and the blue provide a clue
reflected in the traumatized mirror
of the river's flowing to the sea.

V.
The saturated sky
hums a chorus of alien orange liqueur
above the gentle melody of the hills,
windmills like soldiers
in a stick-figure ballet.

VI.
Again the confluence,
not only of rivers but of poet and reader,
of Atman and Brahman,
of blue and plum and
chartreuse and marigold
and pink and peach
that will be carried to the ocean of the mind.

VII.
The fog on the water shrouds a bridge.
To be crossing there,
encased in pervasive uncertainty
in the midst of fleeting beauty.

VIII.
Among the hills
where no one goes
my thoughts meander
aimlessly
this fine morning.

IX.
The ribs of the sky
are like my lover's ribs,
exciting and alive.

Do You Believe in Magic?

Do you believe in magic?
Do you think life is tragic?
Is your approach strategic?
I might ask you seven times
if syllables lead to rhymes.
I might ask you seven more
Whether you are keeping score.

39.

蹇

As Any Animal Must Know
for David Kirby

As any animal must know,
winter is a temporary
affliction that will soon pass.
In the meantime make the most of
the frozen river shortcut
to your warm home along the shore.

The day is dawning cold and clear,
and you will find a sunny spot,
heat up a cup of good cheer,
and open up the book of now
that is a revelation
of your soul's inner equinox

and the recollection of the
future and its many seasons,
facades of reality,
anticipations of past times,
all enfolded into this
momentary sanctuary.

Look out your window at the scene:
the downy woodpecker and the
three sparrows at the feeder.
You need to replenish the seed.
You need to write this poem.
And you will, a little later.

Innocent Clouds Obstruct the View
for Rolando Andrade

Innocent clouds obstruct the view
Of the sunrise and thus create
An oyster-shell-like collage

Of color and unexpected
Beauty, just as in our lives
Obstacles often produce pearls.

This Morning's Version of the Sunrise
for Malcolm McKinney

This morning's version of the sunrise
Is a jackknifed semi in the fog.
Time slows down, the driver eyes
This morning's version of the sunrise,
Invisible ice, a sheet of lies,
An entry scribbled in the log:
"This morning's version of the sunrise
Is a jackknifed semi in the fog."

The Cold Ground
for Cara Lorello

the cold ground beneath
my thinly shoed feet
feels as though it could freeze me

from the ankles up and turn
me into a tree
dreaming of the spring

Sunrise Behind Pines

sunrise behind pines
they like bodyguards
or acolytes of the sun
the distant festivities
reserved for the few
paying customers

school zone when flashing
but it is sunday
so feel free to drive like hell
through the neighborhood with the
sunrise blinding you
on your way to church

yesterday the snow
came down in fat flakes
accumulating ankle
deep and then the sun came out
making melting slush
that then froze again

the road to the sun
is also the road
to and from the hurt and pain
all the winters of your life
laid down as pavement
for your long journey

The Weight of the Sky
for Troy Putney

the weight of the sky
resists the sunrise
but the trees and the mountains

welcome it with a breathing
song of acceptance
in the orange light

40.

解

I Woke to My Heart Fluttering
for Mahdi Meshkatee

i woke to my heart fluttering
this morning the taste of dreams
the weight of old gray skies

i resolved to let it go
that memory that rose
i went up to the roof to see

A Future Sunrise Will Come

for Kayleen Dunson & Catherine Kirkwood

a future sunrise will come
as a sign of deliverance
now we wait but then the sky

will clear of all obstacles
the pink and blue and gold of love
will unfurl across the mountains

When Deliverance Comes
for Karey Lee Perkins

A calm pink and blue sky
sets the scene for a return
to normalcy and light.
There is a change in the air,
a feeling of the mending of
the structure of reality.

The birds in the garden
partake of the poetry
of the replenishment
of the water from the hose
coming from miles and miles away
to sparkle in the rising sun.

Jesus said deliver
us from evil and lead us
not into temptation.
And when deliverance comes
let us relax and enjoy it—
no need to yammer on and on.

Yet we may also speak
and our words may form poems
to describe the rising
and to celebrate the sky.
Let us go then into the day.
And let us go then, you and I.

Variations on a Squirrel
for Michelanne Adams

1.
Up the oak he goes,
A flash of brown, bushy tail.
Dog leaps, barks below,
Fury now a manic dance.
Squirrel laughs from branch above.

2.
The dog he sees a bushy tail,
And up the tree the squirrel does flee.
He's off to chase without a fail!
The dog he sees a bushy tail,
He barks and leaps with joyous hail,
A sight for everyone to see.
The dog he sees a bushy tail,
And up the tree the squirrel does flee.

3.
A blur of fur, white and brown, races
Across the green backyard; the dog's
Gaze fixes on a tree where
A bushy tail flicks high,
Teasing, taunting, just
Beyond the reach
Of the dog's
Bounds and
Leaps.

4.
Hark! What movement in mine eye doth fall?
A flash of grey, a tail of bushy grace,
Up yon tall oak, it doth ascend and call,
A challenge to this wild and merry chase.
My paws do pound upon the verdant ground,
My breath comes fast, my heart with joy doth leap,
No sweeter scent nor sound can e'er be found,
Than this pursuit of secrets I would keep.
Around the trunk, in circles we do spin,
A dizzy dance of hunter and of prey.
Though oft I fail, yet still I hope to win
This furry prize, for with it I would play.
But shouldst thou flee, I'll ever give thee chase,
My noble squirrel, at thine frenetic pace.

Squirrel Sestina

for Lis McDermott

My frenemy the dog
Is quick but not enough
To leap a lying log
And catch me in the rough
As I make a magic twist
Like a dervish in the mist —

A mystic move that's missed
By the boggled brain of dog;
Such an acrobatic twist;
As if that weren't enough;
And his baffled 'ruff ruff ruff'
Scribbled in his Pavlov log …

So he sniffs the latest log
His owner must've missed,
A land mine in the rough
Full of info you could dog
If you just had sense enough
Like a wine snob with a twist.

Ah, but now I give a twist
To this game of tree and log:
I haven't had enough.
A ninja in the mist,
I call out to the dog
In a taunt that's tough and rough.

Again his *ruff ruff ruff*
Comes out but with a twist
Of slobber-of-the-dog
Like slug slime on a log.
But then the branch I missed.
My leap was not enough.

Will I be fast enough?
I land a little rough —
Like a Mrs who has missed,
Playing twister with a twist —
Right behind the log,
To the surprise of dog.

The dog, who's had enough,
Leaps log and mutters, "Ruff?"
I twist — again — he's missed!

The Struggle of the Sun to Rise
for Frederick Fullerton

The struggle of the sun to rise
will be replaced by daylight
and the calm realization
that the second in command
can easily assume the helm
of the day as it progresses

towards a strange and terrible
night of irreducible
stars to guide and deliver
every lost ship to its port
where once again the sun will rise
as it inevitably does.

A Slit of Serious Sunrise

for Tom I. Davis (in memoriam)

A slit of serious sunrise
Above ironic cargo
Nonetheless signifies
Deliverance from, if not
Evil, at least the ossified
Circumstances of the long night.

The Moon

for Sean Singer

The map of the moon on display
against the pale cobalt sky
is what we see: the moon itself
showing its face to the earth
while holding its cold fingers crossed
with dark secrets behind its back.

41.

損

To Increase Is to Decrease
for Maya Zeller

To increase is to decrease.
Waking early means sleeping
less than if you had let yourself
continue in the dark unconscious
of enormous night. To decrease
is to increase with the light:

Waterfowl cross the river,
foraging at the surface
where the gadflies, thick in the air,
falter and fall to be scooped up
with succulents, forbs, and grasses
green under the orange sky.

The Glory of the Sun Decreases
for Debbie Wagner

The glory of the sun decreases
after the slow explosion
of color
        as of a Van Gogh
or a Gauguin—being
poor was how they let the coral
from tubes of paint squeeze out to the end
and fill the whole world, posthumously,
with unanticipated
splendor.
        Just like that, I empty
my pockets and remove
my shoes to pass through the gates of
the dawn, empty and strangely alive
at the tail end of the dying world.

Jettisoning

The harbor master guides you
into your berth along the pier.
With gentleness and grace
you slowly glide into your life,
jettisoning the old past,
grasping my hand as I pull you up.

Half the Books in My Library
for Walter Lindgren

Nine syllables become eight
In the dance of change and decrease
Half the books in my library
And my one love in life
Are all I need at this time
The rivers getting lower

42.

盆

Whatever Progress I Made
for Sam Aureli

Whatever progress I made
this morning was mostly made by
harnessing my carcass to the
sun dimly rising above the
gleefully-green globe willow
reaching out into the faint

increase of warmth in the world
and the thought that while I had slept
a creeping goodness was working
its stealthy music in my bones
like the voice of my daughters
singing to me from the sun.

Dream of My Daughter & My Two Cousins

My daughter has called me
asking for help with her bike
which has a flat tire.

She's stranded with it
somewhere that is reminiscent of
High Drive in Spokane.

I arrive and air up the tire for her.
She rides it about half a block,
as if to test it,

then parks it and gets in the car with me.
"What are you doing?" I say.
"Aren't you going to ride it home now?"

Cut to: the parking lot of Fred Meyer.
Now she and I are both on bikes,
circling around the mostly empty lot.

I pop a wheelie
and go into a wide arcing turn,
leaning back far enough

to brush the palm of my left hand
along the pavement.
It's a bit show-offy.

My daughter tries the same maneuver
and doesn't do too badly
but can't sustain it very long.

She has a look on her face that says:
"I'm just doing my own thing
and I don't care what Dad's doing."

Cut to: the entrance of Fred Meyer.
My daughter and I approach together
but either she doesn't go in

or immediately veers off
to some other part of the store
as I head for the warehouse-like space

of custom-cut carpeting
and lumber and such.
My two favorite troubled cousins

are there waiting for me.
We seem to be involved in some project,
remodeling a house to flip perhaps.

I point out to them how the optics
of the room create an illusion
of it being smaller at one end

than it actually is, which is surprisingly
massive. We walk in that direction,
feeling the space expand.

The Unburning Bush

for Steven & Julia Bovingdon

I get up at four-thirty in the morning
and step into my shorts and flip-flops,
my body aching for no reason,
get in my car and drive down to the river.
A sign says, No Camping, and I wonder
if I'll be mistaken for a camper at this hour.
But there's no one around, just some ducks
swimming upstream, browsing for bugs
and things. I stand next to this bush,
unlike Moses, unlike Jesus, just myself,
and consider the sunrise and the blessed ground

Gazing into the Suburban Fog at Sunrise
for Jerome Young, OSB (in memoriam)

Gazing into the suburban fog at sunrise
I ask the sky to make me wise
To clear the fog of lies
Remove my inner spy's
Disguise
So I
Can lay me down to die
In peace
Among the geese
Perhaps to rise up
In time to size up
The odds I'll win this bet
And get
Home before the sun has set

Sunrise Ghazal

Hazy sunrise on the eastward Selkirks brings me these old dreams.
I hand them to you to sift through like the embers of cold dreams.

My father appeared with his fiddle and beer, my mother
Doing laundry in the next room, obliged by tradition to fold dreams.

My sister aware of the movement of the earth awoke to see
That there may be a way to buy back some of those sold dreams.

My daughters so different arose to the challenge of the sun
To seek their own fortunes and make of the sky their own bold dreams.

My love in the distance so close and so far from my longing
Sends me on sunbeams her diamonds and silver and gold dreams.

And I, Jonathan, alone in the morning begin to be burdened
By joy in the moment of gathering and telling these told dreams.

43.

夬

When I Arrived in Spokane
for Samuel Ligon

When I arrived in Spokane
yesterday without a plan
I stepped out into the gray
unmusic of a gray day,
and yet there was a feeling
under the cloud ceiling

of a murmuring deep down
within the soul of the town
that made me think something had
caused some change to good from bad
or that some deeper resolve
was starting to absolve

the shadows and shine a light
down the tunnel of the night
in which the town had been trapped
while negativity slapped
the faces of the better
angels of our nature

and that now, riding the bus,
those angels were guiding us
towards a tentative dawn
where no one has their guns drawn
and spring and summer follow
the flight of a swallow.

The Continental Divide

Towards the continental divide
From the top of Butte, Montana
There's a seething in the sunrise
And a burgeoning of feeling

As autumn turns into winter
And the time has come to decide:
Will we keep on counting the days
And the time that we've been stealing

Or into the river of surprise
will we throw the calendar
And light a match to the moment
And blow the roof off the ceiling

Because the continent can't hide
The pressure building in our sighs

The Ballad of Franz and Hank
for Garrison Keillor

Kafka and Bukowski
Were coughing over coffee.

Franz said to Hank,
"I breathed instead of drank."

Hank said to Franz,
"I'm allergic to prawns."

(Which they'd also been eating
At this late-night meeting.)

Dream of the Intrusive Stoner

I'm down by the river
in Beaconsfield on a warm
summer day. There are

a few boats coming
and going, and I'm wondering
if I might get someone

to pull me on my
waterskis. I've waded out
with them, hoping

someone with a ski-boat
will see me there and offer.
A long-haired stoner

dude floats up in a
dinghy and says, "Do you
wanna buy some weed?"

"No thanks," I say.
He becomes belligerent.
"Why not?!" he says

emphatically,
almost angrily. "I just
don't care to," I say.

"When was the last time you
had some?" he says. "None of your
fucking business," I say.

I wake up feeling agitated.

Fogbound at Day's Dawn

fogbound at day's dawn
just before winter
begins to claim the river
and the bridges surrender
i hike to the top
of this hill and howl

44.

姤

That Fragment Reflected

past and future sunrises tempt
the early riser to seek
something that doesn't exist

like that fragment reflected
at the bend of the canal
don't let it disrupt your flow

Dream of the Donald at Doggy Daycare

I'm parked outside
the doggy daycare place
near the campus,

either picking up
or dropping off
my dog (who is

somewhat different
from the real-life one).
The car is either

a '70s or '80s era
ramshackle thing
or a futuristic

self-driving thing.
I'm sitting in the passenger seat
which might actually be

the driver's seat
(because I might be
in a British TV show).

Donald Trump appears
and it seems that he
wants to ride with us.

(You're in the backseat
which is also, strangely,
possibly the driver's seat.)

There seems to be nothing
to do but let him
squeeze his corpulent

oversized greasy self
into what would be
the driver's seat

(but seems not to be).
Donald acts friendly
in a menacing way

like a mob boss.
He puts his fat hand on the
console between the seats

and I look down at it
gauging its size and assessing
whether he really has

such small hands—
an allegation that's always struck
me as an undignified

cheap shot.
I rest mine near his
to compare.

The car is moving now.
I look over at him,
somewhat repelled.

He's tossing his usual
word salad
with a side of bullshit.

"So how do you think
you caught the CV?" I say.
And then realizing

no one calls it that,
I correct myself.
"Coronavirus, I mean."

Acknowledgement and Resolution

i.
If I could
I would
Prioritize
Your eyes
Your thighs
The music of
Our love
Our sighs

ii.
In fact
We did enact
This plan
We cracked
The border ban
And ran

True Affection

I was hoping to catch you under the mistletoe
At the Christmas party but you didn't show.
I was wishing I could be with you
In a way that was good and not untrue.
I thought I might find you somewhere,
So I roamed the streets and sniffed the air.
And when I saw you coming out
Of the movie house, I didn't shout.
I said, "Funny meeting you here, I was just on my way
To see that new Nativity play
They're putting on at Our Lady of Hope.
Would you like to come? Nope?"
You said something about wanting to go home.
Your mouth was full of foam.

45.

萃

When It Snowed in New Orleans

for Jeremy Marks

Is Lake Pontchartrain a lake
or is it a mud puddle
on a grand scale that could be
jumped into with both feet to splash
New Orleans with a sazerac
of big muddy mystery?

The meaning of Groundhog Day
might be lost on your Cajun.
Down on the Mississippi
They prefer a creole mix of
the profane and the crazed sacred
leading to a shadow's kiss.

And they prefer to gather
together to celebrate
the basic weirdness of life.
And when it snows—every hundred
years or so—that's just an excuse
for another pride parade.

So let's gather together
for an early Mardi Gras,
my friends, and let's let it be
like nothing Punxsutawney Phil
has ever dreamed of in slumber
but more like his waking up.

Refugees of Morning

for Matthew & Deirdre Lickona

Unpeeling the sunrise like an errant orange
Across the river from Café du Monde,
I and the other refugees of morning
Have gathered here to pay our homage to
The Mississippi and the love left over
From the many plates of love we served
The night before the night before the night
Adventure took us down a path of light
In such a spell of love we were unnerved
To see our names and to discover
Resurrection in some graveyard voodoo,
Some Cajun music and some beads adorning
The dial tone left after you phoned
To announce something wonderful and strange.

The Struggling Sun Well-Risen
for Kevin Taylor

The struggling sun well-risen
looks at me like a glum lover
tired of grinding through the smoke
and grit of another sky
in the grim infinity
of possible skies of August.

Through the trees, we exchange glances,
the sun seeming insubstantial
compared to my solidity,
my own air-conditioned skin
feeling the faint beginning
of the summer's smoldering end.

Dream of Mingling at a Conference

I'm at a conference with my librarian wife
And we're walking among a stream
Of other attendees—in the warm twilight—
Towards the conference hotel where
The closing keynote is about to happen.

Along the sidewalk, we come to
My toiletries bag sitting there in the grass
Where I apparently purposely left it.
I pick it up and pull out the dental floss.
My wife and I continue on, flossing as we walk.

We arrive and stand around chatting—
With each other but also with a couple
Of old librarian ladies. I remark on how much
Our brushing habits have improved.
"We used to hardly ever—well, really never."

My wife cheerily agrees but even as she does
I realize I've grossly exaggerated the case.
I begin to go over in my mind how often
I used to brush. Nine times out of ten?
No, even more frequently than that.

Then I say something about how frequently
I get up to piss at night. It's a casual
conversation and the four of us
Are standing by a metal utility structure
Which I'm leaning on as if at a bar.

Then we all go in, but there's a delay.
The auditorium is dark and empty
Save for a few librarians with lanyards.
The organizer had been waiting but
Decided to go have a drink to kill time.

The Color of Morning
for Daniel Henderson

the color of morning
as a ripening peach
the amble of sunrise
as an old map that changes
take a breath or look away
and suddenly the day begins

46.

升

The Change in the First Line
for Dennis Held

The change in the first line
points to a little sadness
but mostly a feeling of
vitality and adventure
like that of the supple sunrise,
the trees, the rocks, the hills, the wind.

It's the season of growth,
and gradually a growth
in understanding may come.
We may soon come to realize
that many of our certainties
are crumbling beneath our feet.

It is impossible
not to live and not to die.
That's the way of this strange world
in which we find ourselves growing
upward towards a blinding light
and eventually falling

like Icarus, our wings,
our vitality, melting
until we rejoin the earth.
But for now we fly, and Love
provides the muscle and the
music that keeps us aloft.

The Reading of the Sky
for Laura Read

the reading of the sky
echoes with the oracle
telling me to continue

letting myself be drawn upward
by the same gentle force
that brings tulips in spring

This Work
for Zan Agzigian

In the middle of this autumn
that has eased its way into
my humming summer, I will
hold onto my inner springtime
and continue this absurd but
sweet work as best I can.

Like the sunrise I too arise
to ease these lines into life
to let the colours of dawn
stream from my faltering fingers
tapping these keys as the coffee
stirs my blundering brain,

blundering into obstacles
but nonetheless pressing on,
taking a deep breath with the sky,
feeling my bare feet on the floor,
seeing these purple hues emerge
from within and without.

The colours are unnamable
but our task is to name them
or at least to keep trying:
amber-washed, golden-smeared, peach-plunged,
pink silken-fingered wedding dress,
violet ... violet.

Accidental Companions

for Karen Sandberg

The cable bridge and the rising sun
Are my accidental companions
On my way out of town this morning.

I'd planned on an old storehouse gray sky
Filling the railroad cars of my mind
With gray matter, not this sumptuous

Transport of velvet violet and gold
Careening into orange and pink,
My thoughts becoming branches of trees.

Spring Morning Progression
for Anna Greenside

the roof ridge points
to changing skies
where vanishing
geese honk and fly

the scent of buds
faintly floating
in the echo
of their shrill cry

and blood red turns
to amber orange
and cars like waves
pass by pass by

on the highway
by the river
feel the flowing
to the great sea

After Seven Days
for Paul Wittenberger

after seven days
of cabin fever sky
i looked out the window
and saw my golden mansion
inviting me to
rest among the clouds

the swooning branches
of trees delicate
but stern in the brittle chill
of the confrontation with
the air above and
the breezes below

were the rungs of a
ladder my mind climbed
like old jack and his beanstalk
without the fee fi fo fum
and instead carl jung
explaining my dreams

the blue that had been
withheld and the mauve
merging with pink and purple
the necessary angel
of mister stevens
awake in my brain

and the glory of
nature never spent
despite the faithless brooding
pretended under grey sky
until it opens
to reveal the this

and as well i turn
in my ecstatic
thoughts to mary oliver
and her harsh and exciting
wild geese heading home
through this very sky

what else can i say
as emily said
the sky was low the clouds mean
but there is another sky
and we have stumbled
upon it here now

ah that handsome pine
in the back yard stands
now healed of its brokenness
only bending a little
its hallelujah
under the blue sky

and finally i
begin to come to
myself in the looking up
in the crash of cloud and light
and in the music
of the sound of words

I Have Known These Trees
for Mark Anderson

i have known these trees
from afar but now
i wish to drift among them

in the mist of the morning
and feel the sun rise
over the selkirks

I Woke in a Fog
for Julie Miller

i woke in a fog
but made my way up
to a hilltop vantage point
to pay homage to the sun
and share the clarity
with everyone

47.

困

Catching an Early Morning Flight
for Fotini Masika

Catching an early morning flight
with my daughter to visit
her second-choice college,
she on crutches and feeling beat up
by the relentless beat of
a mildly throbbing stress fracture,

I operating on three hours
of sleep due to bad habits
and a distaste for death,
the plane strains, creaks, and groans to lift off,
the collective BMI
of the passengers and their dreams

perhaps too much for the physics
equation someone forgot
to calculate. But soon
the plane has lurched its way to heaven
and I have succumbed to sleep
to dream of my canoe and hers

waiting on the dry-cracked lake bed
of hope, she with her crutches
walking towards the shore
and I following, carrying her
bag full of dreams and anger
to our final destination.

Although I Did Make It Out of Bed
for Alan Girling

Although I did make it out of bed
and out the door in time to hop
on the Lime bike I'd left on the humble corner
across Bernard (to avoid aspersions)
and in time to ride said bike
(graffiti beautifully sullying its flanks)

to the cliff edge above the city's flanks
(which is to say, from the river bed,
the north and south, where, if you bike,
many a bridge will make the hop
from one side to the other, without aspersions,
a pleasant one, from corner to corner) —

yes, although I did go from that corner
powered by my own thighs and flanks
and a bit of lithium ion (aspersions?)
to the sun still lying in her nightly bed
but beginning to kick off the blankets and hop
like the dream or the thought of riding a bike,

I myself rode just such a bike
to the cliff edge near the airborne corner
of Cliff Drive and Ben where a hop
the wrong way could land you in the flanks
of pines and pussywillows and the bed
of some poor homeless fellow's aspersions

not to mention the sprung rhythmic aspersions
of some drunk poet riding a bike
above you in the wee hours out of bed,
but yes I stood at that corner
(the bike exhibiting its stunning flanks)
at the earliest hour a man could hop

out of bed and into clothes and then to hop
onto a bike and to ride through the aspersions
of the uncertainty which certainly flanks
the sun as it lifts me and my bike
like a scene from the VHS (from the corner
Blockbuster Video) of E.T. (out of bed)

to see the sky as a bed and to hop
off (like turning a corner from aspersions
to love) and then bike to morning's blue flanks.

The Fog Refused to Lift
for Rod Bluhm

The fog refused to lift
This morning at the break of broken day.
The cable bridge in darkness lay.
Between the sky and water stood a rift

Of dark solidities adrift
And soft soliloquies of words to say
The fog refused to lift
This morning at the break of broken day.

I felt myself begin to sift
Into the river's sway
Through foggy spaces of my time away
From sunlight and the morning's gift
The fog refused to lift.

The Broken Limbs
for Mary Pierce

The broken limbs and whispered hymns
Of river ice beneath which swims
The fish of long-forgotten dreams
Once caught, then lost, as failure seems
The sunrise where with frozen whims

My frostbite fingers splinter shims
And clouds from which sun-blindness dims
These words on paper stacked in reams:
The broken limbs.

And so my mind skates round the rims
Of cups in which hot coffee brims
And floating clots of sweetened creams
Feed stupid thoughts of silly memes
While winds whip up and snow-wisp skims
The broken limbs.

Autumn River Sunrise Triptych
for Alan Lautensleger (in memoriam)

The morning light, the taste of tears,
The unseen sun, the feel of frost
Against your face up to your ears.
The morning light, the taste of tears,
The sounds of things that no one hears
Like ships out on the ocean tossed,
The morning light, the taste of tears,
The unseen sun, the feel of frost.

Grizzled the Morning
for Derek Annis

grizzled the morning
takes on airs of gray
and i become a gray man

standing on the gray doorstep
of a gray heaven
looking for the sun

Phantom Sunrise

phantom sunrise
like a missing limb
within my own horizon
memory of sunrises
haunting the winter
like an unsung hymn

48.

井

My Treasure Chest of Old Journals
for Joan Hue

My treasure chest of old journals
is a wellspring I dug deep
when I was a young river,
to find my soul's tributaries
and fresh water for my mind
when I awoke in the desert.

The open vein of ink I spilled
into that well grew into
a darkling moonlit pool,
purified subterranean
music fed by minerals—
my treasure chest of old journals.

And in my chest, my breathing lungs
and beating heart make music
I can dip into at will
and drink a cup kindness yet
and hear the ocean waving
my river forward rounding third.

That's where I am, just rounding third
but staring into the well
and hearing the ocean there
whispering its deepest secrets,
the ones I told and tucked into
my treasure chest of old journals.

The Dig

I need to dig your soil with my hands,
to excavate the contours of you,
my fingers carefully finding the

roots of your thoughts and the routes of your
undriven disciplines, the secret
subterranean recipes and

sacred burial places of your
beloved dead, silent sonatas
of mystical muscle memory,

the archaeology of every
moment in the movement of your now,
your placid piano birdsong soul,

the intricate treasure box of—the
ancient coins and artifacts of—you.

Dream of Sedation

I'm laid out
on an exam table
in a doctor's office—

not a full-on hospital.
Sedation has been
administered and I'm

beginning to feel
it, but also feeling
some nasal congestion.

The doctor comes in—
a semi-obese, friendly fellow
with dark curly hair

and a dark beard. He
asks if I'm feeling any
nasal congestion

because that could be
a problem for the procedure.
I say that yes in fact I am.

I'm feeling some worry
verging on panic
as I fade to black.

The Grandmother

for Janice Lindgren

The grandmother emerged from another
dimension stitching realities together
from the depths of her being,
the gathering dark of antimatter
at her back, the morning light of her
childhood streaming in the window,
her sewing machine in actuality a
time machine, the lenses of her glasses
ground down to thin membranes of air,
memories slowly gobbling up the future,
dreams quickly creating dancing partners,
a rapid procession of rejected
suitors, and an epic telephone call
connecting her to a bright new world.

The Gently Falling Rain
for Jane & Thomas Grassadonia

My father would have been eighty-four today.
I imagine him standing here beside me
observing this tenuous, delicately
beautiful sunrise with its pink-against-gray
lattice of light projecting from a burning
arc as if God's about to weld the heavens
shut, or, conversely, as if the Sacred Heart's
about to burst through and blow reality
to blessèd smithereens. I turn to see him
smiling at this fancy with a look of love
as he fades into the gently falling rain.

What Molecules Move
for Christine Myres

what molecules move
through the veiny leaves
of the trees and how i ask

animal exhalations
plus water drawn up
to breathe with the sun

River Graffiti

for Paul Lindholdt

river graffiti
reflected in fog
luminous gloominess

soothing my moodiness
waterfowl follow
the sunken sunrise

The Moon This Morning
for Erin & Raleigh Brown

the moon this morning
made a bright moaning
above the whistling wind
merging with the dark keening
of the cold creatures
deep in the river

49.

革

The Great Reset

for Nick Ripatrazone

The risen sun revealing
a postmodern passion play of
cardinals and jays urging
me to slug down my coffee
and join them in the chaos
of the great reset of the day.

Courage to Radically Change
for Josie B. Lash

courage to radically change
may be required tomorrow
now is the time to prepare

consider the chaos to come
be ready to ride the wave
coming beyond the horizon

The Season of the Change-Up
for Roland Brown

1.
The season of the change-up
is upon us, with sliders, curves,
and off-speed pitches blooming
in the air or darting like
swallows in the magic zone
between the sunrise and home plate.

2.
Rarely is there bad weather
at the ballpark, just constant change
sometimes erupting into
base hits, other times easing
into a dance-like rhythm—
to be shattered by a homerun.

Molting
for Kim Nelson

Waiting for the washer and dryer
to be delivered—the last step
in the process of moving
that has had us in its grip
like a slo-mo full nelson
these past several weeks—

we sit here at sunrise, my mother
and I, with our cups of coffee
and a fresh breeze blowing in
through the old screen door made new,
the trickery of April
playing out in the sky.

The house and life that are left behind,
the narrowing down and shrugging
off of so much while so much
remains in the storage room
below our feet, such a large
space to hold memories

half-remembered in fragmentary
pieces held tight while letting go.
And now into that large room
the washer and dryer will
also go, hoisted downstairs
by muscular young men.

Rain Falling on the River
for Chanda & Derek Neu

rain falling on the river,
the same river but never
the same, the sunrise stretching
like a bridge beneath the clouds,
the same sunrise but never
the same, the rain not raining
very hard, the sun rising

God Is a Train Car Graffiti Artist
for Mark Rico

god is a train car graffiti artist
jesus is a two-lane interstate road
the angels dance on the telephone lines
the devils drive the cars in front of you
holy mary is a road sign you can't
quite read up ahead and the sunrise
is a secret gleaming in the headlights
of the oncoming traffic but writ large
in the feeling in your feet when you get
out and walk and breathe in the morning light

Riding Backwards on a Train

Riding backwards on a train
In the morning with my love
Slogging through the fog of pain
Riding backwards on a train
Through the fog into the rain
A naked hand inside a glove
Riding backwards on a train
In the morning with my love

When we arrive the sun breaks through
The sea of people parts for us
We can feel that it is true
When we arrive the sun breaks through
The songs that play for me and you
Remind us not to make a fuss
When we arrive the sun breaks through
The sea of people parts for us

You go to work, I climb the stairs
Up to my mountaintop retreat
We disavow that no one cares
You go to work, I climb the stairs
The Lord receives our subway prayers
The air outside is fresh and sweet
You go to work, I climb the stairs
Up to my mountaintop retreat

What Is This For?

What is this for?
I asked the man
who handed me
a golden knob.
He just pointed
across the room:
a knobless door.

50.

鼎

The Open Field
for David Poff

The open field where dogs must yield
To every scent and every sound
As light spreads out across the ground
Is where I've ventured to be healed
Of human thoughts, to drop the shield
Of human ego where I found
The open field.

As dawn erupts, what was concealed
Becomes apparent to my hound
Who wags his tail and runs around
The plot of land where I have kneeled:
The open field.

The Ponderosa

for Sherman Alexie

1.
the ponderosa
pines on high drive bluff
prickle the frost that shivers
invisibly in the air
the needles of the
limbs hum in the sun

2.
the sun doesn't rise
so much as emerge
like strange flavors poured onto
a sno-cone in the summer
orange and yellow
near the carousel

3.
the frosty asphalt
beneath my sockless
feet inside my new snow boots
awaits the snow like a man
determined to stand
in the winter sun

4.
tallest pine where the
bluff slopes down toward
the railroad tracks and highway
that go to places I've been
and places I've not
my eyes slurp the sky

5.
hangman creek it's called
flows down there under
this savage sunrise after
the atrocity george wright
committed when he
hanged chief qualchan there

6.
this ponderosa
in front of me is
a witness of the winter
that hangs ready in the air
even as the sun
recalls the summer

7.
the ground beneath me
slopes away from me
beyond broken history
my brother ponderosa
chief of the pine trees
breathes the sunrise air

8.
yellow is golden
intensely glowing
beyond our ability
to grasp it fading into
the great beyond of
orange and purple

9.
take a deep breath and
another feel the
frost in your nostrils the sun
on your tongue see the landscape
and your place in it
turn and face the day

I Was a Lineman
for Christopher Howell

Out on the ridge line underneath the wind
That blew the clouds into the rising sun,
I made my rounds to see what I could find.

I was a lineman called to check the bend
Of voltage where the lines were getting thin
Out on the ridge line underneath the wind.

A report of conductor gallop where they spanned
From tower numbers six and eight and ten
Meant I would have to see what I could find.

So I drove the bucket truck out to the end
Of highway eighty-two to put it in
Out on the ridge line underneath the wind.

The lines weren't dancing hard enough to mind
So I parked and watched the dawn as it began.
I'd made my rounds and reported what I found.

The wind kept pushing the gold-laced clouds around.
The sun came up, its power on my skin
Out on the ridge line underneath the wind.
I drove away to see what else I'd find.

In Magical Ink
for Paula Clark

I.
I rode my bike in the dim light
Of predawn to the riverbank
Where the sunrise was in preflight,
The river filling up its tank
With all the drinks I ever drank.
Tipsy ducks were having a lark
Catching critters before they sank
Into the river deep and dark.

II.
A local pelican flew over
On a lonely reconnaissance
Of the sunrise river scene,
Gliding through the orange,
Strange, and beautiful
Late summer air
On the wings
Of the
Dawn.

III.
I felt myself subsumed into this world
Where light and water and color and air
Mixed together, momentarily swirled
In such a way I began to cease to care
About my anxiety and despair,
Instead embracing a feeling of love
That nudged the political push and shove
Into the river to bubble and sink
Into the murky depths while up above
This poem appeared in magical ink.

The Glassy River

for Sharma Shields & Simeon Mills

The glassy river moving still,
Its lucid dreams adrift until
The sun infuses everything
With strange intensity. I sing
A silent song as if I will

Retreat into the gentle spill
Of dreamy thoughts that gently fill
The morning and its secret spring,
The glassy river.

Someday we all must pay the bill
For what we've done. Not shrill
The bells that day will ring
And nature heal the broken wing,
The sun arising to fulfill
The glassy river.

This River Brings Time
for Richard & Mary Ann Vogt

this river brings time
from the mountain streams
irrigating the farmlands

with the minutes and the hours
of the dawns and dusks
of eternity

In the Beginning
for Caprice Buck

in the beginning
of the day open
your eyes and breathe in

deeply and then let your breath
out naturally
as the sun rises

51.

震

The Harbormaster
for Jed Moffitt

The calm of this sunrise scene
masks the shock, terror, and laughter
that lingers, muted, in the dawn.
The quiet boats here anchored
contain a cargo of trembling
carried over from the big bang.

A calamity of wealth
afflicts the shopping cart of dawn:
the remembrance of the fading
season, remembered as if
gone even before it has left,
loss and grief anticipated.

Yet in the fading echo
of the explosion of summer
there is a substratum of mirth,
a settling of the earth
into a placid smile and hum
and heart vibrating like a drum.

The harbor's undulations
and the way the boats bob in the waves
tug at the harbormaster's heart
and incite the thought that we
are all the same harbormaster
and the harbor and the sunrise.

Dream of the Toaster & the Armed Women
for Viola Weinhold

I was staying in a house, by way of refuge.
It was night and I was outside in front of the garage.
I had a toaster on a little table and was making toast

when suddenly several armed women appeared,
dressed in black and wielding handguns.
In my haste to get my toast out before they shot me,

I tipped over the toaster, a sleek old silver and black one.
I was struggling with a butter knife, trying to get my toast,
which I felt was very important.

Then I realized they weren't interested in shooting me
but were rather pointing and shooting
at something or someone inside the garage.

The Mountains East of Bozeman Town

The mountains east of Bozeman town
Present the sunrise with a wall
To climb up on and never down,
Like putting on a wedding gown
To wear to some frontiersman's ball
That's broken by a battle call,
A tidal wave that comes to drown
The mountains, hills, and people, all.

Dawn Came Down Like Dust

for Armin Vogt, Sr.

This morning dawn came down like dust
Cascading from the grinding sun.
I said to someone that I trust,
This morning dawn came down like dust.
My eyes were sleepy, full of rust.
Perhaps, she said, the summer's done.
This morning dawn came down like dust
Cascading from the grinding sun.

Six Haiku at Sunrise

for Jason McBride

1.
Wires stretched across the
horrible beautiful sky,
sending love and hate.

2.
Utility pole,
electric crucifix, stands
in the blood-orange air.

3.
Globe willow next door,
revived from traumatic death,
buds in the sunrise.

4.
My neighborhood sky
stretching to infinity,
blue, orange, pink, gold.

5.
The sun itself clears
the cold horizon and shoots
its rays through bruised clouds.

6.
My window open,
the cold morning air strangely
suffused with warm thoughts.

My Nine Lives

1.
At the age of eight or nine my cousin Brad
and I, having learned you could break open
firecrackers and make a free-form sparkling fire
with the gunpowder inside, decided to take it
a step further. We located some large-caliber
shells of my father's, took them out on the back
patio, got a hammer, and proceeded to try
to break them open. Unsuccessfully.
We gave up. With an odd, goofy feeling,
I found my father in the living room and held
out my hand to show him the bent shells.
His eyes widened and his face turned pale.

2.
A few years later, I'd discovered skateboarding.
I was getting fairly adept by then, though nothing
like what would come later with ramps and pools
and punk rock and flying high. But still
I was daring enough to set up a bar for jumping
over—the skateboarding equivalent of a high jump—
incrementally raising the bar higher
and higher till I caught my toe on it and the bar
didn't budge. My forehead collided straight on,
like a hammer, with the concrete floor of the garage.
Later, I knocked myself out again but with a helmet on.
And broke my collar bone. But all in all not too bad.

3.
Then I also got into karate and attended a training
in Ellensburg with my fellow karateka, Kerry.
It was a hard training, something like boot camp,
and by the end of it we were tired teenagers.
We were driving home through the desert
in an El Camino, I driving, Kerry sleeping shotgun,
when I started seeing my eyelid curtain falling.
Next thing you know, we both wake up, the El Camino
sliding bumpily at high speed on the sloped shoulder
of the highway, chunky railroad-track gravel grabbing
at the tires, one hub cab flying off into the sagebrush,
Kerry crying out, "Slow down! Slow down!"

4.
I learned to fly an airplane and flew it with
my sister to yet another karate training,
this time in Boise. On the return trip over
the mountains of Eastern Oregon, I knew a storm
was brewing above the mountaintops as we
approached, and I knew better than to do
what I did, which was to throw caution to the wind
and continue on instead of landing in Baker
and waiting it out. In the thick of the mountains
I also found myself in the thick of the storm clouds,
bouncing through the sky with my worried sister,
following a mountain road below and holding on.

5.
Unsafe at any speed. Driving my pickpup
back to college after Thanksgiving, an early
snow covered the highway, I in a hurry
to get to class, daydreaming about Alan,
who'd fallen asleep back in the spring
on the same stretch of the road I had — but died —
when I suddenly realized I was bearing down on the car
up ahead. Feeling my brakes a little, I could tell
I had no snowball's chance in hell of slowing down.
So I began to pass and went into a slide,
sideways in slow motion past the little car,
then sliding wildly again, a semi barreling towards me.

6.
Again in the same truck two years later,
out of college now and living in Seattle,
negotiating my morning commute down I-5,
shoulder to shoulder with others, all going
as fast as we possibly can, when one of my front
wheels collapses, folding under due to what
I'm later told was a bad ball-joint, and wrenching
my truck out of its lane and into the path
of death once again. Do you believe
In guardian angels? If there are such beings
I've been keeping mine pretty busy. I find
myself parked somehow, out of harm's way.

7.
A few years went by with no near-death experiences.
I doubt that, though. I imagine there were a few
that I either wasn't aware of or that I've forgotten.
Like getting pneumonia when I had no insurance
or the two rainy Seattle fender benders
I was in that might've been much worse.
I lived a precarious existence back then which probably
caused me to be more cautious than otherwise
within the context of my overarching recklessness.
Suffice it to say, I count myself lucky to have survived
this period with my life intact, in addition to
the more dramatic episodes described above.
To God or the universe or my lucky stars I give thanks.

8.
But I wasn't done with this chess match with Death.
When was it—ten years ago now perhaps?—that I rode
my bike to work and upon completing the day
was coasting out of the parking lot, which sloped down
to the street. Stupidly, I decided I should reach down
with my right hand and tuck my pantleg into my sock—
while continuing to coast along, my speed gradually
increasing with the increase of the slope.
With my left hand I applied the brake. It grabbed
and my front wheel locked. I didn't know what.
In half a blink, I flew over the handle bars and landed
directly on the top of my head. Oh helmet! Oh!

9.
Am I running out of lives? Here we are
at number nine. I could cite a time or two
driving with my daughters while they learned
when we saw our lives flash before us, but let's
leave that aside and just give thanks for the alarming
wonder of being alive for the time being.
And continue to hope for the best. Safety First
is a motto I've sometimes ignored but will try
to observe more diligently in the days to come.
Meanwhile, friends, take care but not too much care,
I say. For, like the poet said, life's not a paragraph
(and death, methinks, is no parenthesis).

There Can Be No Why
for Helge Busch

there can be no why
in the economy of
the ongoing autumn sky

because all the whys are made
irrelevant by
the sun's blinding what

---

es kann kein warum
geben in der ökonomie
des fortwährenden herbsthimmels

denn alle warums
werden durch die blendende
sonne unerheblich

Shakespeare, Too

Shakespeare, too, counted syllables, but he
also imposed a pattern of stresses—
most often iambic pentameter.
(That's not what these lines are illustrating.)

52.

艮

The Moon Reflects the Unseen Sun
for Rick Jones (in memoriam)

The moon reflects the unseen sun
around the time of the sunrise
or what would be the sunrise
if it could be seen. But relax,
resist the urge to speak
when you have nothing to say

about the onset of winter
and the darkening of the day
as sleep becomes a harbor
in the chilly wind of dark thoughts
and a soft bed of dream
invites you to hibernate

so that, forgetting all your cares,
you enter a lucid landscape
of eternal memories,
a reversal of miseries
as you feel your way through
the things you had been scorning

and heal through the dismal morning
until the wonder of the world
again takes you unawares
and you are captive of the joy
that your own silence brings
when silence secretly sings.

Meditation

for David Ell

The sun rises by keeping still—
A model of meditation.
Think again. The whole solar
System is speeding through space at
Five hundred thousand miles per hour—
This morning's meditation.

The Pines
for Christopher Robin Lyman (in memoriam)

The pines
That stand
The pains
That blend
With bliss
And hope
To pass
And shape
The dawn
Of day's
Refrain
Of haze
To raise
The dead

The Place You Find Yourself

for Glenn Siekawitch

Life is a crazy quilt of tombstones and rowhouses
and if you're lucky a lighthouse to break up
the monotony, to give you a point of reference
to get your bearings and perhaps climb to the top of
to survey the scene, to see the orchards for the trees.
The world is a collision of intentions
meeting at the borders of compromise
accidentally blessing each other with the surprise
of apostrophes and stitches and hyphens and children
as if punctuation and syllables might hold hands
and radio music overlapping with conversation
and laughter might coalesce into the pattern
of a communal symphony organically arising
to a crescendo of the pursuit of happiness.
The place you find yourself is a place from which
you can grow wings and take flight
to see it all as if through the eyepiece
of a kaleidoscope or the euphoria of having
fallen in love until you fall back down not too gently
to your almost forgotten place in the clarified confusion
to live the remainder of your days
waiting for what comes next.

Sunrise Through the Sagebrush
for Wendy Gray

sunrise through the sagebrush
dry grass in the golden light
the momentary lush
vision of the end of night
that tells me all shall be all right
as i listen for the hush
beneath the urge to rush
beneath the rush to bite
into the apple of the day
into the words that people say
the music of my breath
the calm of life the calm of death
the sunrise in my eye
and miles to go before i die

Taking the Long View
for Erin & Alvin Green

taking the long view
of what you see now
might just mean relaxing to

let what's happening happen
take a breath and let
it out as clouds drift by

53.

漸

As One Word Follows Another
for Rory Waters

As one word follows another,
so I follow my heart's promptings,
sometimes slowly sometimes fast
but always at a steady pace
that keeps time with the music
always playing within me.

Early This Morning

for Natalie Waters

I.
Early this morning
I woke to the night
Surrendering to the sun
As it does every morning
I woke to the sun's
Generosity

II.
From the backyard of
My awakening
I saw the past and future
Making friends with the river
I saw the sky spread out
Its enormous arms

III.
My mind climbed the tree
Its dangling limbs
Inviting me to defy
Gravity and common sense
My soul floated down
The canal of dreams

IV.
A car on the road
Flashed a wink at me
As it knowingly passed by
To some strange destination
As the driver looked
To the gentle dawn

V.
And I was left with
This unending song
Filling up my breathing lungs
Carrying me on towards
The one who loves me
And waits patiently

High Drive's Your Best Bet

High Drive's your best bet for viewing the sunrise
In the winter months in old Spokane. The bluffs
Stretch out below you with pines receding down
To the tracks and Hangman Creek, the highway
That goes past pieces of my past,
Spangle and Plaza and the rolling Palouse hills.

This morning, I look at the sky above those hills
With colors that announce the coming sunrise
And foretell a mostly blue-sky day though past,
Well past, the point of freezing, when winter's bluffs
In the seasonal poker game go down the highway
With all your cash pocketed in the goose down.

The truth is I'm feeling just a bit down—
The winter blues—and I wish I could wander the hills
All the way to the border and find a hidden highway
To make my crossing under the warming sunrise
To where we'd have our house up on some bluffs
Overlooking the Gulf of Mexico and boats sailing past.

I wish I could seize hold of our separate past
And make it connect from here all the way down
To the eternal verities where God or the universe bluffs
Us into thinking there's gold hidden in the hills
When in fact it's beaming down from sunrise to sunrise
And it's under our fleeing wheels, paving the highway.

What I really want is to be driving down that highway
With you riding shotgun, pulling our trailer of the past
Towards the new and long-awaited golden sunrise
Of the mysterious future filled up and weighed down
With the fullness of our beautiful present, the hills
Of Eastern Washington colliding with heaven's bluffs

Where you and I will accept the morning's bluffs
As the sky becomes an orange highway
With coffee-colored clouds above the green hills
Of the coming spring and the present zooming past.
We'll drive that golden road all the way down
To Pullman and beyond to an as yet unknown sunrise.

I'll hold your sunrise hand as we recall these bluffs,
The arrowleaf balsam down along the winding highway,
Creating our new past from these memories of the hills.

Long-Distance Love Song

1.

From this upstairs room in America
I hear the noise of cars on the highway.
I know the river is there beyond that,
Flowing silently down from Canada,
The mysterious country of your sleep.
The vast and uninhabited country
Where I could sleepwalk a thousand miles
Never stepping in a waking footprint.
If the world crumbles into night, I will,
According to our plan, and we will meet
Halfway there in Vermillion Bay and sleep.

2.

Lucky is the night
When it dreams of you
Silent is the night
As I join your sleep
Soon will be the night

When I lie with you
Distantly the Night
Heron makes its cry
Easy is the night
When the morning light

Finds you in my arms
When we wake to see
The light surrounding
Our distant bodies
Emerging from dreams

Gracious is the night
To give way to sight
To bring us the day
To open our eyes
Softly you and me

Morning my woman
Bonjour mon amour
Lucky the man and
Lucky I am to
Be waking with you

3.

Missing your body here
The smell of you, your hair
Tickling my nose, my hand
Traversing your gently
Rolling hills, valleys, your
Mouth in the dark, and mine

4.

I'd shoot the lights out for you
In the lighting department
Of Home Depot on a slow
Night when store security
Least expected it, not to
Cause any harm but only
To let you sleep in my arms

5.

In the not too distant
Future I will fly to you
In a gravity-defying
Contraption filled with sleeping people

And people reading books
And watching flickering screens
And sometimes looking out windows
Like me daydreaming in-flight of you

6.

You are sleeping as I write this
I'll be sleeping as you read this
My sleeping mind about to dream
Your dreaming mind freshly woken
Both our minds infatuated
With the dreams that move between us
And move us both to awaken
As if kissed and gently shaken

My Long Travel Day

My long travel day and the winter blues
left me longing to lie with you
without my shoes, my naked feet
bumping into yours like lines on the street
disappearing under broken lights,
like an unrehearsed magic show,
like some word I can't quite
remember but am sure I know

quite well. Quite well, my love, quite well.
Like I love you. Like Je t'aime.
Like you are and like I am
as we navigate the morning bells
to catch the sunrise and the train,
smiling through the edge of pain.

Burns Night Revisited

"I committed the sin of Rhyme and fell in love."
—Robert Burns

I was making midair turns
While reading Robbie Burns
Thinking of my bonnie bride
Who'd soon be giving me a ride
Home from the airport
For poetry and loving sport.

54.

歸妹

My Lady of My River Dreams

for Lynn Martin

Rising with your crown of gold,
My lady of my river dreams,
Awaken in my sleeping friends
Awareness of their broken hearts.

The blessings that you've sent my way
Are hard to catch and hard to hold,
But here I am with arms outstretched
To touch your skirt as the day starts.

Like starting fresh when one book ends,
If I could double all I see,
I'd read again into the dusk
And pay no heed to missing parts.

But now I feel a hint of cold
And see beyond the river's bends.

The Pettiness of Pathetically Underpaid Poets

I believe there should be a universal basic income
for poets and that the definition of poet should
include everyone.

If there must be a test, let it be that you have
the ability to breathe, either on your own,
or with assistance.

Let's call that a haiku and if you'd like to write
an actual haiku then go ahead and do that, but,
even so, you are a poet.

If you are alive and sentient and can breathe
then you qualify for the universal basic income
I here propose.

And what amount shall this universal basic income
for poets be? I say let it be equal to what members
of the U.S. Congress are paid.

We the people are poets, I say, and provide
value to the world with each breath we take
and each breath we release.

So let the squabbling among the so-called poets
cease and let the prizes and publications be
used to line the cages of birds

And let those birds fly free, too, yes, set the poets,
which is to say, the people, and the birds, but the people,
yes, set the people free. (And the birds.)

The Border Closure

the border closure
blossoms with closed books
and incompatible bills

my mind wanders over the
land crossing checkpoints
pointing me to you

i want to land there
precisely where you
were and will be and are now

in the land i once only
dreamed impossibly
of in my deepest mind

which i now inhabit with
you and your people
somehow strangely true

and yet the border
closure climbs the walls
of my mind your hands touching

my face my eyes seeing you
our salvation here
between you and me

The Slow and Steady Sun

for Luke Ross (in memoriam)

the slow and steady sun
seems to rise as the planet turns
not a mechanical grind

of manipulated movement
but an effortless poem
spoken in a single breath

55.

剝

The Treachery of the Sun
for Ashley & Troy Ross

The treachery of the sun
rising over the railroad tracks
and the gravel and scraped snow
of seven in the morning
is that it casts a thought of warmth
across the dismal train station
and infuses the blue sky
with the feeling of spring coming
even as the bitter cold
makes your eyes begin to weep
and the winter storm announcement
makes tomorrow and tomorrow
and its promises to keep
increasingly impossible.
Now the train is late as well
and commuters have arrived
for the next train, causing this one's
cargo of lives to strain and swell.
We're all in this together,
though, it seems, and we will get there,
wherever *there* is and how
long it takes to gather up
the remnants of our intentions
with our shadows and inventions.

The Skies Cleared Over London

for Jonathan Johnson

The skies cleared over London
to allow us our rising sun
alongside Regent's Canal
running past Thomas Lord's Cricket Ground
to the Prince Regent's park—
the son of the original

stable genius, George III.
As I waited for the fullness
of its rising, I pondered
the Clash song about the immigrants
stealing the hubcaps of
respected gentlemen—and dons.

Let's leave all that aside, though—
along with the Bob Dylan song
questioning how many ears
one man must have before he can hear
people cry—and turn our
attention to the poetry

of John Keats and the bus ride
to the poet's house in Hampstead
where he lived in the fullness
of his poetic genius, writing
Ode to a Nightingale
by a plum tree in the garden.

Inwardly Free of Sorrow
for Shann Ray

Inwardly free of sorrow,
the sun radiates its fullness
to the sheltering morning
as the verdicts of wisdom shine forth
and the dull-wittedness
of the deceptive is revealed
in the sudden early light
of summer colliding with spring,
and the location of dawn
on the eastern horizon inches
to its maximum point
in the land of the midnight sun.
I wake from a solid sleep
with the aching bones of old age
hinting to my youthful mind
that I, too, am approaching that point
where the fullness of life
turns back to glide towards the grave
and the pigeons of morning
celebrate the alternating
sun and cloud and wind and rain
as one journey ends and another
begins, as poetry
speaks to marrow, free of sorrow.

Manic Sapphic

Monday evening cascading down on Tuesday,
Manic sapphic syllables dance from the dexterous
Tongues of poets playing on ancient rhythms—
    Cadences gliding.

Tuesday morning stressing the summer warming,
Global, fetal, walking the dog while talking,
Getting ready to drive from my hive, surviving,
    Overly heated.

Wednesday panics on the horizon, packing for
Thursday, Friday, when my beloved's flying
Frenzy lands her right where I'm waiting in manly
    Readiness calmly.

Daytime, nighttime, everything happens. Lovely
Sappho muses melodies lovers lavish
Forwards, backwards, every which way and bending
    Time with each other.

Garrulous Serious October
for James Mohr

Garrulous serious October
Conceals the sunrise in its gray garments,
Invites you to be both drunk and sober
At the same time while the remnants
Of summer float away in shallow streams
And tasks at hand begin to seem like dreams.

The World Inside You

the world inside you
is a reflection
of the universe beyond
your skin and yet one with it
the same reflection
reflected again

56.

旅

The Sky Is Crazy With Swallows
for Carole Newman

The sky is crazy with swallows,
purple martins writing jagged
lines across the complicated clouds,
feasting at the pinnacle
of their northward travels
here on the island of Montreal.

Like them I too am a migrant
and though I can take my best shot
and likely find that I am able
to bring the king a pheasant
for his table and so
prove myself a capable fellow

I also need to beware of
my tendency for recklessness,
wheeling about the sky of my mind
like these martins, pronouncing
and mispronouncing words
and failing to put on winter tires

when the seasonal change arrives
and the time for caution comes down.
That is the mixed message I receive
this morning among the birds —
while on the horizon
wandering clouds tell me not to fear.

Los Angeles
dozzina

At the age of sixteen, I first traveled
To the city of the angels, with some friends.
Like me, they were skaters and seeking the thrill
We found on curved concrete and ocean waves.
They were there to get high and celebrate
The end of high school, and I was there
To get serious and compete for a pool-riding prize
At Lakewood Skatepark, towards the end of its life.
My friend Todd, over beer the night before
The event, suggested I should use
My martial arts training to calm my nerves
And find my inner California flow

To carry me through the contest's flow
Without missing a trick, and win the prize:
Bragging rights & a first-place trophy that traveled
Back to Washington with me before
Skateboarding almost died, when even the thrill
Of Tony Alva faded out so that he had to use
The coins under his floormats & bits of food there
To survive the early '90s and celebrate
Skating's rebirth in X-Game waves—
But not until many a skatepark owner's nerves
Had been sorely tested and skating life
Had turned to backyard ramps with friends.

When next I recall visiting L.A., it was friends
Living in Pasadena that caused my flow
To channel south in search of an elusive prize:
The nuns of Mount St. Mary's chanting there
The O Antiphons in the silken vocal waves
I'd read about in *Cloister Walk* and the thrill
Of drawing close to mysteries that used
To hide in the Hollywood Hills before
The swirling hurricanes of fire traveled
Through like Hell's angels meaning to celebrate
The destruction of angelic life,
Doing damage to contemplative nerves.

I was thirty-two years old and my nerves
Had grown somewhat taut from their
Entanglement with heartstrings & from standing before
What felt like a strange & useless life.
Thus I arrived & stepped into the L.A. flow
And felt the weather a cause to celebrate,
With the light that flowed in particles & waves
Landing on my eyes like a paradise surprise
I didn't quite know how to use
But found I could enjoy with my friends
Sitting out on their patio as the ebb & flow
Of the Pacific Ocean induced a gentle thrill

To be alive within the California thrill
And the California calming of my nerves.
In years that followed, I found myself flow
Through & around L.A. as I traveled
By rail, by car, by plane, with family and friends,
Still in search of some kind of missing prize,
The Coast Starlight taking me from rainy life
Up north, through Oregon & down to the golden waves
Of Santa Monica to momentarily celebrate
The ocean before lying down then and there
Under the sun & over the moon before
The sunset pointed me to thoughts I could use

To create a map of the future and recuse
Myself from the self-recriminations of my life
And its many doubts lingering there
Until I could vicariously celebrate
The charms of the happiest place on earth before
The childhood of my children escaped the flow
Of Caribbean pirates & Indiana Jones's nerves
Jolting with the twists & turns of friends
Enjoying the rides together & the thrill
Of Tinkerbell & Peter Pan, the prize
Of parenthood with many vacations traveled
Where memory paves the radio waves

Of the fondest times & the simulated waves
Of rollercoaster rides reliving the endless thrill
Of the yin & yang of life here & there
And the repeated wish to win the prize
And somehow grasp the good life
Others seem to have effortlessly traveled,
The illusions created by Facebook friends
And the times when it all gets on one's nerves
And you can't keep drinking from the firehose flow
And you've used up every trick you could use
To pretend to laugh & sing & celebrate
The time before the time before.

All of that happened long before
The dawning of a strange convergence of friends
Celebrating their wedding day and the use
Of UCLA's facilities in a scene that unnerves
My sense of synchronicity's *there is no there*
Like some shadowed nut Jung might prise
From a California shell & the latent thrill
Of surrendering to unusual crisscrossing waves
When you've given in and traveled
To begin a reckless rearrangement of life,
Allowing love's unfettered flow
And your decision to succumb to celebrate

A new life with angels seeming to celebrate
The dangerous sparks and sudden overuse
Of too many *you've got a lot of nerve*s
And violations of poetic license before
Simply embracing the high-intensity flow
And gently caressing unexpected waves
Leading us on a downhill walk to celebrate
Mass at St. Monica's as if we traveled
From the far corners just to go there
After experiencing thrill after thrill
And a picnic near the pier among angelic friends
Witnessing the beginning of a luminous new life.

Fast forward to the navigation of this life.
If I am a pebble, my daughters are the waves
That ripple out from the splash I celebrate
Life with, generally speaking, and the mysterious reuse
Of my blood & DNA that has strangely traveled
The Washington & Oregon coastlines before,
Metaphorically speaking, entering the flow
Of California's highly energized nerves
And the city of Los Angeles the prize
To be shared with them and their friends,
To observe the gigantic & majestic thrill
Of the Hollywood sign & the hills seen from there.

Then there was the cherished trip we took there
With my girls & my parents a couple of years before
My father took his angelic leave of this life.
We stayed in Huntington Beach and followed the flow
To the surfing school where we caught some waves
And watched my father capture the video to celebrate.
Another time in Redondo, having traveled
From pale-skin winter land, the thrill
Of the sun turned into the sunburn of fiends
With licking tongues turning delight into the abuse
Of skin sizzled red down to the very nerves—
Not the hoped-for spring-break suntan prize.

And now Los Angeles is burning its own prize
Like a twenty-dollar bill it can no longer use,
Holding it up like a mad poet to his friends
In a gesture of despair that masks a thrill
Of ferocious fire weather and raw nerves
That bring Lynchean nightmares to vivid life
And death across Pacific Palisades before
The devilish gale-force Santa Anna flow
Begins to subside leaving nothing there
But ashes on sea foam and breaking waves
And no place to gather to celebrate
The end of the fire on the streets that it traveled.

My memories traveled back to L.A. with my friends.
I recall the thrill of Lakewood, the smell of the waves.
I celebrate my many memories of being there.
Let the angels of now bless the prize of this life
Because nothing will be as it was before & we could use
A miracle & nerves like raindrops starting to flow.

The Roulette Wheel of Life's Changes

The roulette wheel of life's changes
is like a bit of bumpy air
on an otherwise smooth flight.
The plan is to venture far
from home and land on red or black—
either one will be just fine.

It seems that we are embarking
on a journey of mystery
requiring humility
and acceptance of the new
and neglected sunrises of
these beautiful future days

encircled by improbable
synchronicities yet to come
and yet already present
in the breathing of the day
as I wander alongside you,
alert to every change.

Riding My Bike to the Library in the Rain
for Bruce Greeley

I've decided to
ride my bike in the rain to
return some books to

the nearest branch of
the local community
public library.

It isn't raining
that hard, just a light drizzle,
not too terribly

cold either. My light
and somewhat reflective rain
jacket is enough

to keep me warm as
I pedal through the gray air,
only wishing my

glasses were equipped
with mini windshield wipers
like ones I recall

from certain ads in
the back of the comic books
of my bike-riding

youth. It is starting
to get dark but I wanted
to burn off some fat

and I wagered I
could mostly ride on sidewalks —
since no one would be

walking in the rain —
and thus avoid commuters
in cars that would run

me down in the blink
of a rain-dazzled eye. I
placed the overdue

books in my rucksack
and embarked Don Quixote
like with earbuds in

my ears playing a
book called *Drive Your Plow
Over the Bones of

the Dead* — the title
a Blake reference I have yet
to look up, the book

recommended by
my wife who reads ten books to
my one, the bike a

heavy beast I bought
for cheap some years ago, the
rain a rarity

in the arid clime
of Kennewick, Washington.
The wry narrator,

a whimsy-worn old
Polish woman who lives in
the Czech border zone,

is talking about
"testosterone autism"
and I'm wondering

if I'm starting to
come down with it, along with
a host of other

maladies common
to white-guy late-middle-age.
Being a poet

inoculates me
to a degree, I think, but
not entirely.

And now I arrive
at the library and drop
the books in the book

drop. Then take a quick
look at the discards the Friends
of the Library

are offering at
prices approaching zero.
I grab *Moby Dick*

And a couple of
others, drop a couple of
bucks in the cash box,

clean my glasses, get
back on my bike, and head for
home. The drizzle

has fizzled and the
air is clean and glistening.
I take a different

route back, down a street
that takes me past a strange house
with a small pasture

for a large front yard
and in it two big brown cows
behind a little

wire fence along
the sidewalk I'm traversing.
The bigger cow takes

an interest and starts
running alongside my bike,
bounding like the whale

to my Ahab, my
bike gliding across the
oceanic world

to the end of the
yard where it seems she might jump
over the fence and

join me to journey
with another jump over
the moon and back home

where I'll tuck her in
and read her some *Moby Dick*
till the cows come home.

God Made Me a Rambling Man

god made me a rambling man
but everywhere the rising sun
greets me like a good old friend

my beloved beside me
is the mountain to my fire
as the sunrise comes and goes

The Days Lining Up Like Birds
for Marty Smith

The focus of the present
is to share this moment
of mystery with someone,
your traveling companion
and guide to good manners,
perhaps, on this strange journey
into the vastness of
tomorrow and the day
after the day after that,
the days lining up like birds
on a wire preparing
to fly away one by one
as you trace their flight paths
across the horizons
of their inevitable
migrations to lands unknown,
to places barely born
and yet eternally old,
which is why you must not
let trivialities
come between you and the prize
lurking in the here and now,
the gold nugget of love
already in your pocket.

Born to Be Borne

> *for Donald Hawkins & Polly Powell*

The sun comes up on my day of departure.
Soon I'll be chasing it to its setting in the west.
But for now I linger with it here at its rising,
The river spreading itself out at my feet,
The clouds creating a second horizon
And a casually billowing blanket of beauty,
Cloud creatures on display and who's to say
Not conscious of their movements—their
Shadows and light and chromatic subtleties—
Creatures born to be borne on the upper breezes
And then to die and to be reborn for pure
Delight. And then the sun, oh, the sun
Commanding attention and burning dangerously
Like the beast of Bethlehem, the ghost of the future.

Dream of Going Back to College
for Elizabeth & Thomas Burman

I am wandering
around a college campus,
an amalgam of—

or an alternate
reality collage of—
several campuses

I've experienced
in my non-dream waking life—
or some version of

somewhere else—feeling
out of place. It's the run up
to finals. Students

(all so young and free)
are crowded into common
areas, indoors

and out, studying
more or less studiously.
You get the picture.

I have my MacBook
and am looking for a spot
to work, but feeling

put off by the crowds
and my age. I approach the
snack bar counter of

a dark interior
and lay down a dollar bill
(among three or four

I have on me), get
four quarters from the pretty
student barista

and at the same time
realize I didn't really
need coins. There had been

some reason for it
(parking meter?) but
I'd paid with an app.

I move on, clutching
the quarters, and suddenly
panic about the

whereabouts of my
MacBook. But not to worry—
It's here. I stumble

out into the light,
onto the lawn of the quad
or whatever it's

called here. Someone, as
a joke to relieve the stress
of finals, has put

socks on a dog and
trained him to sit still in a
pose that makes him look

like a human with
arms stretched out and leaning back,
knees drawn up in front—

and a weird dog's head.
Haha. I continue on,
not finding a spot.

57.

巽

Above the River
for Carmen Westcott

above the river the clouds drift
blue curds in a curdled cup
across the cusp of morning

allowing themselves to receive
the broken sun still hidden
the gentle revelation

The Sun Above, the Sun Below
for Istiaq Mohammad

The sun above, the sun below,
Gently singing on the wind,
Softly reaching to the roots
Of trees providing pleasant shade
To animals breathing here
In a great exchange of breath.

The eldest daughter is the sun
Who sings with the birds of dawn,
Coaxing the shadows to dance
With reflections in the canal
And waterfowl floating down
Beneath the whisps of the wind.

Down on the highway, people pass,
Oblivious to the dawn
And the poem they are in.
They pass right through these syllables
Like molecules of breathing,
Like particles/waves of light.

Meanwhile the sun keeps happening
Beyond their thoughts and wishes,
Slowly filling the whole sky
With its irresistible light,
With its irrefutable,
Undefinable power.

This is happening all around
Us as our thoughts are carried
On the breezes of our lives,
Clearing space for a sudden gust
Of reality to shake
Us awake in a moment.

A white pickup truck emerges
From the black night of the past
Into the early light of
The orange, yellow, and blue dawn.
Who's driving it? Maybe you,
On your way to find yourself.

You arrive on the wind and step
Out into it like Adam
Waking up missing a rib.
You feel the sun warming the day
As you walk towards the door.
Someone you love opens it.

Three Surreal Haiku
with a nod to Stevens' "Sunday Morning"

I.
Clouds like a peignoir
Pigeoning across the sky
During the sermon

II.
Icarus popping
Pills in the boudoir during
The long homily

III.
Getting email from
The bird man of Alcatraz
Through the pipe organ

Frog's Departure

When Frog flew back to his abode
He sent a final text to Toad
To bid his adieu
Before the plane flew
And he had to turn on airplane mode

Sunrise on the Firth

sunrise on the firth
at the end of earth
in the early sunlit north

solstice on the river forth
these words in my mouth
sunrise moving south

58.

大畜

There May Be an Ideal Lake
for Bill Jardee

There may be an ideal lake
(see the concept of platonic form)
hovering above the broken,
beautiful reality
of the lake that splashes at our feet,
that we feel in the end-of-summer

sunrise now breaking into
colour and warmth, with an awareness
of the doubling bubbling
up from the source of all things,
perpetuating a joyousness
like that of the youngest daughter

held aloft by the father
and flung with joy for a splash landing
on the liquid surface of things
as the September flowing
brings its laughter towards October
where there's serious work to do

and where evaporation
of remorse rekindles rainbows' rain
and the kind of hope that doubles
despite the sun's journey south
and the inevitable setbacks
that this joy, too, shall overcome.

Past the Halfway Point
for Deborah Owens

past the halfway point
to nowhere i go
in search of the broken day

for some reason happiness
wells up inside the
cracked bowl of my soul

59.

涣

All Obstacles Dissolve in Time
for Roger Hawcroft

All obstacles dissolve in time
and become dust in the wind —
to quote that old song by Kansas.
The sun at dawn dissolves
into a vast scattering of light
like Dorothy's synapses

caught up in the whirlwind of Oz
the morning after she left
that cow town and shook the dust off
her ruby red slippers
with their glittered unreality
dazzling her dreaming eyes.

That's how I felt when the sunrise
pulled me out of my warm bed
like a mystical tornado
and set me down beside
the steelhead-flanked flow of the river
to simply watch and listen.

My inner cowardly lion
began to roar with the dawn
and I woke to the bright morning
of the imagining
of honeymoons in the soft wet sand
and no more dust in the wind.

New Orleans Sestina

for Jonathan & Tiffany Webb

The sun beyond the Crescent City Connection
Rises on the muddy Mississippi delta
As a barge goes gliding by in search of cargo
And lonely seabirds float and then take flight
To try their luck upstream or perhaps
Resort to plundering garbage bins

On Tchoupitoulas Street, where bins
Are overflowing like a bad connection
In a busy airport where perhaps
Some hapless traveler on a redeye Delta
Scrambled in useless panic to miss the flight
While baggage got tossed in with the wrong cargo

Headed for some conveyor belt where the cargo
Of lost souls drifts dreamily by and the bins
You put your shoes in when your flight
Is at the gate and your phone loses its connection
As you grope for it muttering *bravo charlie delta*
To yourself from the dream you had perhaps

Last night in which there were perhaps
A host of seemingly random symbols like the cargo
Of your unconscious mind converging in the delta
Factor struck by Walker Percy whose Covington bins
Contained the manuscripts of a missed connection,
So he thought, when imagination had taken flight

And a masterpiece of Southern Lit, like the flight
Of a lost Pelican or Richard Widmark perhaps
In *Panic in the Streets* with its public health connection,
Or fill in the blanks with your own cargo
Of dreams stashed away in attic bins,
The alpha, the omega, and, in between, the delta,

Which Percy called the breakthrough into delta
Dawn, the sudden awakening into the flight
Of language, where words become like bins
Of glory, carrying shared meaning, perhaps,
Fantastic pieces of illuminated cargo
Gazed upon and forming an electrified connection

Of I and thou, a connection like sunrise on the delta
Shared in the cargo of a poem taking flight
From New Orleans perhaps in ghostly bins.

Song to the Ocean

I am a river with a tongue but no mouth,
no lips to protect my kisses from their logic,
and I follow a tiresome line of reasoning
through the desert flats and city sharps
of a song I explain but never sing.

Ocean, forgive me. Open your shore to me
and put a new song upon new lips.

The Morning Creeps In
for Robert Pringle

The morning creeps in
And the sun also rises
The coffee seeps in
And we don our disguises

And the sun also rises
The music of daylight
And we don our disguises
We take flight or look for a fight

The music of daylight
Invites us to dance
We take flight or look for a fight
Or hope that some chance

Invites us to dance
The morning creeps in
As we try to advance
And the coffee seeps in

Haiku Epitaph

for Doug & Alyson Wayman

recall the poet
whose name was writ in water
as the clouds drift by

Lever du Soleil

for Nicole Kennedy & Larry Waters

lever du soleil
sur le saint-laurent
mon amour à la maison

birds and clouds adrift across
the bilingual sky
au petit matin

rising of the sun
on the saint lawrence
my love back at home asleep

les oiseaux et nuages volent
dans le ciel bilingue
in early morning

Sunrise Filtered Through the Mist
for Corey Smith

sunrise filtered through the mist
along the alsea river,
the morning becoming light,
the darkness becoming day
by gradual variations,
autumn preparing for death,
death preparing for the night

Museum of the Eternal Now
for David MacGregor

What can this sunrise on the Saint-Laurent tell
us about the particular moment
of time we are living in? Poetry is,
perhaps, a museum of the eternal
Now, wherein the theories of a multiverse
are proven, as if the hands of a gifted
physiotherapist caressed the language
into a sublime rapprochement of meanings
colliding with painful political leanings
to arrive at a multitude of love. One
love that survives many grievances to thrive.

Dear People of the River
for Thomas & Honor Webb

dear people of the river
this river and every river
and people of the sunrise
this sunrise and every sunrise
whether visible or hidden
we are in process dear people
and what a strange process it is
we wake to sleep
as we tumble towards the sea
we rise to shine
as we embrace the inevitable darkness
that never overcomes us

A Windy Morning on the River
for Carole Roseland

A windy morning on the river.
I walk the wind of the cable bridge
from the Pasco side out over the water.

My back to the wind, I face the east,
looking out at the old railroad bridge,
a vestige of the colonial invasion

that started with Lewis and Clark
and continues apace with housing developments
springing up in the desert where I make

my rounds with fast food deliveries
to white folks and brown folks
and gray ones in the dim light.

I handed a fiver to a young man
with a cardboard sign I didn't read
who told me about trying to retrieve

his stuff from the sheriff and not having
much luck. Good luck, I said, and:
I love you. I surprised myself saying that

and I wonder if he, too, was surprised
or shocked by my reflexive expression
of some kind of kindness as I continued

on my way to this sunrise so shockingly
gorgeous in the wind.

At Six O'Clock in the Morning

at six o'clock in the morning
i went down to the water
to look out upon the risen sun
after a long gray string
of cold wet days disappearing
into forgetfulness

60.

節

Where Not To

for Amelia Waters-Côté & Tyler Crawley

Silence is a limiting factor
beneath the surface of the frozen
lake reflecting the sun
as if the quality of warmth
has been extracted and sunk
below the appearance of it.

Roethke said to learn by going where
to go, but sometimes it's where not to.
As I stood on the ice,
frozen solid enough in the
minus-twenty-one morning
for the danger of falling through

to be inconsequential, I still
felt the cold claw of death on my face,
I still wondered if I
Shouldn't have remained reclining
like a leisurely potted
plant in the greenhouse of my room.

That was yesterday and indeed I
am glad I went out on the ice then.
But today I have learned
the limits of my world, and stay
within the warm confines of
my sunstrewn heated living room.

Dream of a Bob Dylan Seminar
for Patrick Muir

I'm attending a seminar
given by Bob Dylan in an old
high school classroom somewhere.

It's a large empty room
with lacquered hardwood floors—
as in a gymnasium.

There are about twenty of us
sitting on the floor around Bob,
who is seated on a stool

in the middle of the room
with his guitar. He's singing
something like "Visions of Johanna"

and occasionally grabbing a harmonica
and sticking it in his mouth.
There's a harmonica holder dangling

around his neck but he's not using it,
instead clenching the harmonica
between his teeth while playing it.

He finishes the song,
sets the harmonica aside,
and starts talking. I've stretched out

in a supine position on the floor
in front of him and he's glancing
down at me. He doesn't directly

address me but he says something
that seems to be an oblique
chastisement, something like:

"You should always try to remain
upright." I take it under advisement
and remain supine.

Dream of Bob Dylan Preaching

I'm in church and Bob Dylan is preaching.
I'm having trouble finding a seat.
I'm about to find one
after squeezing down an aisle,
when a woman with a big
winter coat shifts over into it.
I show my exasperation

a little and go all the way
to the front to circle back around
to the other side. People
are looking at me. Walking back
up the side aisle—I don't know
if people have scooted over
to accommodate me or what

but suddenly there are big gaps
in the pews and plenty of room.
The pews are big antique brown
leather affairs. Bob is sporting
frayed jeans like teenage girls wear.
He's younger, not the eighty-year-old,
more like in his twenties.

He's saying, "One person, I need
one person." He's walking around
in the aisles with a wireless mic
rather than standing in the pulpit.
People are scuttling around.
I take my seat and try to glare
at the woman who prevented me
from sitting, but I can't catch her eye.

The Alchemy Of

the alchemy of
the frozen path to
the felt reality of
my fingers in and out of
the warmth of my glove
the river of love

61.

中孚

I Could Spend My Life Along the River
for Rex & Sharon Flaucher

I could spend my life along the river
Wondering what each day might deliver.
I could watch the waterfowl meander
In the flow protected by their dander.
I could stand here staring out at where
The hidden sun is coming up, aware
Of nothing pressing in but only bless
This feeling of a blessed loneliness.
And when the gears of time take hold,
I could feel the winter's coming cold
And walk to where a fire is crackling
With warm hands and sparkling
Eyes that seek me out as I also seek
Nothing and everything and words to speak.

Vienna
dozzina

I went there in my youth to train my body
In martial arts at Hanshi's dojo, hidden
From sight unless you knew the way to look
Down Lerchenfelder Straße, deep within
The building, fairly small and somewhat humble;
A room or two and a little courtyard lawn
Where Isao and Nobuo led their students
In kata, stretching, partner training, talk
Of bodhisattvas, angels, astral travel,
The auras and the energies of light
Emitted from the punches and the kicks,
The blocks and throws and self-defensive tricks—

Vienna's sleeves so full of vintage tricks.
And then I went to college for its body
Of knowledge, reading other books for kicks
When I was shirking my assignments, hidden
In Penrose' winding stacks, tracing light,
Enrolled in German, hoping for a look
Abroad, a stint of study and of travel,
To be among the bells again within
The churches and the sounds of foreign talk.
I thought the plan was set but then the humble
Occasions of money trouble faced by students
Afflicted me as I crossed the college lawn.

My year abroad was spent mowing the lawn
And working swing-shift jobs and turning tricks
Like buying motorcycles and selling them to students
Or taking them for rides: the student body
Adores that sort of thing and I was humble
Enough to start their motors with my kicks.
Vienna faded in my mumbled talk
Drowned out by conversations hidden
Between the pages of the books within
My basement bedroom, its dim light
Still burning paths away that I might travel
If only I could open up my eyes to look.

For forty years I didn't think to look
Towards Vienna, I just mowed the lawn
Again and shelved that thought's forgotten travel,
Instead pursuing other travel tricks
And breaking things I couldn't fix, like light
Bulbs and marriages, graduate students'
Neurotic obfuscations blanked within
Opinionated ghost without a body,
Confirmation in the church of hidden
Unbroken lineages of strange and humble
Monastic silence cluttered up with talk
Of parenting and children, playground kicks

Resulting in the goads against which kicks
One's soul so as to take a second look.
Vienna fell back into view with talk
Of taking the March break on Schönbrunn's lawn,
To follow on the heels of Paris, humble
Vienna's Wienerschnitzel and Schnapps, to travel
There and to converge in Mozart's hidden
Kaleidoscope of operatic tricks;
To feel, after separation, meine Liebhaberin's body
And wake in jet-lag stupor late in light
Relying on the coffee's fix within
My brain to wake me up like students

Astride their Lipizzaner stallions, students
Who have to stay alert, avoiding kicks
When walking through the horses' stables within
The Hofburg palace where onlookers look
At cutlery and dishes glinting light
Behind the glass in corridors of talk.
The average tourist with aching body,
Constricting muscles for hours, locates a lawn
And there reclines—and other travelers' tricks,
Like finding an off-the-beaten-track and humble
Taverne with some Bier und Brot hidden
Away on a side street off the road more travel.

And back in time like Freud the travelers travel
To see a monument defaced by students
Of history: Lueger's Schande no longer hidden,
Graffiti-painted metaphoric kicks
To the antisemite's groin (despite the humble
Ignaz Mandl's mentorship within
The district where handsome Karl learned the tricks
Of local politics). They liked his look,
The ladies did, and watched him on the lawn
Or in the ballroom filled with crystal light
Waltzing like a man with godlike body,
Infusing Jewish Questions in his talk.

The mayor inspired Hitler with his talk—
Who lived there at the time but would travel
To Germany and there assemble a body
Of zealous psychopaths and brainwashed students—
Resulting in the murder of the light
By Nazis and by "countless Austrians" hidden
Behind respectable statues on the lawn
Where deportation, theft, and torturers' kicks
Have now become a wall of names to look
Up loved ones lost in the Shoah, humble
Children, women, and men whose lives by tricks
Of evil vanished, darkness growing within.

Vienna has that ugly stain within
And no amount of optimistic talk
Erases blood, no clever magic tricks
Can make it disappear, but we can travel
Around the giant ferris wheel's humble,
Slow, circuitous transit and feel our body
Recover from those times and sneak a look.
We all can learn to be like woken students,
Or like a football player when she kicks
A ball at seemingly the speed of light
Across a cosmic democratic lawn
To where the truth has always been hidden.

A side street where Shakespeare & Company is hidden—
Not equal to the Paris one, but within
Are ladders and books to the ceiling; outside, no lawn,
Just pavement and stairs descending like the talk
Germanic tongues produce describing light,
The way the light and shadows can play tricks
On bloodshot eyes when everyone who kicks
Some habit, like the constant urge to travel,
Begins to settle down like a room full of students
In the Albertina studying the ardent humble
Chagall perhaps or finding something to look
At like Hoffer's Girl with Record, her body

Revealed in part and not unlike the body
Of some neo-classical subject hidden
Behind a modern vinyl record. Look
At how the war has worn her down within.
Outside, the weather is typical of March—humble
Pigeons perch in bunches above the lawn
Surrounding a monument to Goethe, students
From a kindergarten laugh and talk,
It's warm when the sun shines but when clouds travel
Over and breezes blow, inadequate light
And cold air unite, the wind chill kicks
Its heels up till the sun does one of its tricks,

Revealing itself above medieval tricks
Of massive engineering like the body
Of Stephansdom laid out with a boot that kicks
The sky, the south tower rarely hidden
From view when wandering in and out of light
And shadow, rounding curving streets to look
At wonders of history brought forward by time travel,
Stumbling on Beethoven, Strauss, and Mozart within
The music of a polyphony of talk
Pervading the rustling almost springtime humble
Return of birdsong and buds and tired students
On break from their exams, resting on a lawn.

My aging body feels the future hidden
When I look down Lerchenfelder Straße and within
My past, my humble tries and unmowed lawn,
Recalling fellow students' cheerful talk
About Klimt's kiss and how to travel light,
How love and time are full of kicks and tricks.

Dream of Hang Gliding with My Mother

My mother and I are flying together
in a hang glider above the Columbia River
and the desert of the Columbia Basin.

We see an enormous flock of seagulls
rising up against the backdrop
of slate gray late winter sky.

So I lean to wheel the glider around
for a better look and then we see
An equally formidable kettle of hawks.

It looks as though a rumble is about
to take place, like Westside Story,
and I'm picturing blood and feathers flying.

But then I realize we're losing altitude.
I forget about the rumble in the sky
and I look down at the arid earth below.

I kick my legs a bit, hoping
to catch a thermal or an upward current,
but all I feel is a helpless sinking.

Our descent is gentle but irrevocable
and now I see several wolves
running along a wide path

directly below us. We're so low
now that I can extend my foot
and pat one of the wolves on the head.

I think about it a moment and then do so.
The wolf looks up at us and perhaps the sight
of this amiable old woman next to me

stirs up a concomitant amiability
in him and he seems to understand;
his look is friendly and unsurprised.

The wolf continues trotting along
but moves out of our way and we
make a clear and uneventful landing.

Later, I find myself back at the house.
My daughter is there and I'm telling her
the tale, but her grandmother is not there.

We got separated after the landing and
she went to see the seagulls and hawks.
I reach for my phone to call her but

it's her phone I've set on the table —
they got switched. So how will I reach her?
I suppose I'll go find her or she'll find me.

62.

小過

The Dignity of the Morning
for Mary Locke

The dignity of the morning
Bathed in beauty persists all day.
In my mind, I float downstream
To my golden destiny,
But I know reality may
Be filled with small obstacles.

The river's currents won't always
Keep up with the pace of my dreams.
Dark details of many nights
May intervene between me
And the bright dusk I imagine
On the vast and stately ocean.

The Lone Wood Duck Before the Waves

for Kim Stafford

The lone wood duck before the waves
In the early morning of my
Day when small things may be done—
Like dredging my memory
For small clues from the past pointing
Me to new possibility.

The Squirrels
for Rebecca Snow

The squirrels have built their home among the falling
leaves of the darkening branches of the fall
just as I have built my home in the calling
of these words laid out in lines that call
my name as if recited from a tombstone
obscured with the leaves of many an autumn
or spoken into the speaker of an old phone
or into a well that seems to have no bottom
and yet allows the sound of an echoing splash
when you drop a pebble in or a coin
whenever you make a wish to lose some cash
or seek a friendly group to let you join,
and the last leaf of the highest thinnest limb
clings to the sunrise sky like a silent hymn.

Sunrise Solo Sestina

for Brian Funke

i once soloed a plane over this basin,
once upon a time, and wants, a pawn,
a thyme (parsley, sage, rosemary and)
a few thousand sunrises ago
when my brain wasn't fully formed
and the rivers didn't say where they were going.

I gave myself a capital I while going
Off to college—not Columbia Basin,
But a more expensive one that formed
The basis for eventually having to pawn
My license for something I'd had long ago,
Long before either/or turned into both/and.

but for the short while i had a Cessna and
two Pipers to fly i felt myself going
higher and higher and further ago
than i could remember as i washed in the basin
of my dorm/hospital room up on
what felt like a hill—but feelings misinformed.

There I was a freshman there to be formed
By the study of the Great Works of the West and
Perhaps a nod to the East like a pawn
Glancing at the sunrise going, going,
Gone, like water swirling in the basin
And going down the drain of long ago.

remember me to one who ages ago
played that record in my room and formed
this memory before i gave up, went for a base on
balls and called it good, Joe DiMaggio and
his gal who'd got up at dawn and were going
to redeem everything I'd had to pawn.

But there I was in the air, riding high upon
The clouds, my instructor from long ago
With the pair of scissors he was going
To use to cut the back of my shirt which formed
A traditional keepsake suitable for framing and
Putting on the wall or to sponge out a basin

after shaving in that basin; a clean-shaven pawn
Going off to college and giving it a go,
the dawn newly formed, and going, going, gone.

It's Not a Matter of Flying
for Matthew & Sheri Hiefield

It's not a matter of flying
but of climbing up the mountain
to greet the sun ascending,
step by step, making the most
of the moment-by-moment change
and the light laying out your path.

Let your footsteps drip with the light
and let the cool of the morning
embrace your breath as you go
with dignity but without
grand intentions or greedy goals
but only appreciation.

It's not a matter of hitting
grand slam home runs every minute
or of calling thunderbolts
down onto the mountaintop
but only to feel soft thunder
within your heartbeat as you climb.

This carpet of gold spreading out
behind you as you continue
on is meant to tell you your
footsteps are blessed and your way
is clear all the way up to where
the thunder rumbles the thin air.

63.

既濟

Preparing for an Interview
for Richard Westcott

Preparing for an interview
with a view of the sunrise,
itself calmly undertaking
to fill up the day with light,
I interrogate the river
to translate the sky for me.

Having slept hard most of the night,
I wake to pull myself up
by the dangling chains of the moon
slipped free of night's gravity
on its way to the horizon,
the river's words on my lips.

Now is not the time for grand dreams
but only to be awake.

The Morning Is Like a Cat
for Randall Ferry

The morning is like a cat
moving with stealth and nonchalance
across the backyard of sky
while I watch from behind the glass
of the French doors looking out
upon the scene of dark changing to light.

It is a Saturday scene.
The world still wants to be asleep,
and most of it is. I want
clarity to come crashing down
in a benevolent stomp
that shakes the world to wakefulness.

Let the established order
be jostled again to chaos,
from which we must assemble
a new reality from this
complacent bland inertia,
from these worn-out puzzle pieces.

Let the water above boil—
not boil over onto the dawn,
but boil to a proper heat
to be poured over coffee grounds
to spur the black cat of dawn
to leap forth with claws extended.

A Favorable Outlook

A favorable outlook
is foretold in this morning's dawn,
but the delicate balance
of sharing a pot of coffee
could also conceal a knife
waiting in the shadowy light
to reach around in embrace
and plunge point-first into the back
of the unsuspecting day.
So beware, you early risers.
Watch for betrayal at noon
and disinformation at night
as the evening drains of light
and autumn leaves begin to turn
the colors of the sunset.
Beware, you people whose roses
will have bloomed all summer long
when the last ghostly petal falls.
Long before that, as you boil
water for your morning coffee,
do not become distracted
but keep a close eye on the pot,
with thoughts of the garden plot,
and then pour it over gladly.

Near the Confluence

    for George Perkins (in memoriam)

Near the confluence of the Yakima
And the mighty Columbia, the sun
Is setting over the teeth of a saw
Biting into the day soon to be done,
And the night soon to begin, a rerun
Of the night before and the day that dawned
Before that, when, rising from bed, I yawned
And pulled the curtain open in my room
For a view of the parking lot and, beyond
That, the future strange as an empty tomb.

The Broken Line in the Sky
for Gary Spangler

The broken line in the sky
after completion of the dawn
points to the hither and yon,
the limited supply
of mercy in these mean times,
the unpunished crimes

it's better not to look at
in the rear-view mirror as you
drive into the false and true,
the white dog and black cat
of the future witnessing
the all-encompassing

change at what seems like the end
but that is a new beginning
after losing then winning
because around the bend
there's no telling what you'll find
letting the day unwind.

Don't let the pause in your breath
become a loss of momentum,
a clenching of your sternum
that halts you unto death;
keep the line from going slack,
keep moving, don't look back.

The Frozen River

the frozen river
continues flowing
deep in its reality
quantum nonlocality
taking me away
bringing me to you

64.

未
濟

Nearing Completion

Stepping up onto the shore,
your lips meet mine, softly and fine,
and then we stride to the steps
of the mountain and surrender
to its heights, and then descend
to new puzzles and mysteries.

Saffron Blackberry Sunrise
for Vanessa Waters

A saffron blackberry sunrise
above the ungainly sweet
potato shaped lump of land set
down to divide the flow of
Kaniatarowanenneh
on its way to the great sea.

There's something different in the air
this morning, a turning point,
not the finish line but the thought
of a new world and this one
changing, changing, no turning back,
everything the same but new.

The river, the birds, the beaver—
all seem tuned in to this change,
this change to what remains the same.
The river is eddying,
the birds are gliding and swinging
in higher arcs than before.

I see the beaver lift its head
above the surface to look
at me and then to dive again
to the secret places there
along the shore, using its tail
to tell me a secret tale.

Walking on Water, Holding Fire
for Carolyne Wright

Walking on water, holding fire,
I turn to myself and ask
a thousand questions in one sigh,
addressing the oracle
sky, bowing wearily to wait
for my final instruction.

I had been here a thousand times
before, before arriving
here for the last time this last time.
I've used many instruments,
scientific and musical,
to provide an alibi.

But now, finally, I am near
the point of a new departure
like an old fox on thin ice
in the springtime of an old year,
nearing the end of my journey,
carefully approaching shore.

For the end of every journey
is the beginning of one,
and I dare not fall through before
I make it to the bright shore
where the sunrise is welcoming
me with its beautiful fire.

The Blazers
for Thomas Gasior

sunrise from our pearl
district hotel roof
rip city crows cut capers

in the caterwauling wind
the sun coming up
a hail mary shot

Why

for Lorraine Evanoff

The sun comes up and filtered through the smoke
Appears declawed, a strangely ruby red
Serene and glassy orb a wizard's cloak
Reveals within its folds. The letter zed
Some geese fly by and form across the sky
Disquieting the morning with their harsh
Exciting search for home—the question Why
Do I exist, or you or them? awash
Against the hazy wonder of the hills,
The atmospheric orange horizon blending
With distant longings, urges, strange quadrilles
Of colors, clothing, cards, and dances ending
Just as the day kicks in, the spell is broken,
The ordinary words of morning now are spoken.

Dream of the Biology Speech
for Kurt & Kelly Lash

Spring break is over
and everyone has to give
a speech in Biology.

I wrote mine some time ago
but misplaced it
so when I am called on,

I wing it. The class period
ends before I am finished.
The next day the professor

says to the class, "Now is
your chance to volunteer
and get it over with."

(For the longest time
the room has been silent
and even after he says this

still no one speaks.)
"Perhaps I should go," I say,
"Since I left off yesterday

and maybe my speech
is still fresh in everyone's mind."
I cringe at how badly I said that

but then think, well,
it wasn't that bad,
it could've been worse.

The professor appears to be
slightly professorially offended.
"Either that or you should wait

till the very end," he says
as if it is self-evident
I should wait

till the very end.
"But, as no one has volunteered ...."
So I begin my speech.

Or begin to begin.
I stand up and face the class,
but I can't for the life of me

remember where I left off
yesterday or even what
I was talking about.

"Well ..." I say,
thinking hard. "Hmm ...."
Then, finally: "I can't

seem to remember
where I left off.
Did anyone take notes?"

There occurs a general
thumbing through
notebook pages and

shaking of heads.
They don't have any better
clue than I.

One girl, however,
a smarty-pants type,
pipes up and eagerly reads

a sentence which I recognize
to be not from my own speech
(the content of which

continues to elude me)
but from the professor's
closing comments of the day before.

The professor,
sitting nearby, shows me
a xeroxed sheet

with the sentence just
recited by my classmate.
She got one of the words wrong.

Armed with that
superior knowledge
but still unable to recall

anything about my speech,
I launch into it, thinking
I will use anything I can recall

from *The Neck of the Giraffe*.
I repeat the sentence,
using the correct word,

having no clue
as to its meaning, adding
something like,

"... as so-and-so just
quoted from Professor ...
Professor ..."

(but I can't remember
the professor's name)
"... the professor's comments

of yesterday."
Then I begin to talk
about the New Biology

and about how efforts
to come up with a new
evolutionary theory

have taken on a rather
pseudo-scientific or even
religious quality.

Another professor
has stood up, enthusiastic
about my message

but wanting me
to get on with it,
and added his two cents.

Suddenly the classroom
is outside.
A road

passes the back
of what would have been
the room.

I have to raise my voice
as noisy cars drive by.
Several men jog by,

some carrying
newspapers
or rolled up magazines.

They seem to exemplify
some point I'm making.
Class ends.

I have taken up
the whole period
and didn't even

get in a conclusion.
But I can't help feeling
it was a success.

Still Asleep I Leap
for Thomas Caraway

still asleep i leap
from my bed into
the confusion of the day
the sun just risen and blue
sky surrounding
white and gold and green

white van and black truck
nose to nose in snow
the driveway and sidewalk clear
the zen scene of yang and yin
squaring off under
a late winter sun

on high drive a car
affixes its beams
on me perhaps driverless
as if doubting the sunrise
and i look beyond
to the gold-rush sky

i hazard to stand
in the middle ice
refrozen on the asphalt
and feel the possible cars
rumbling out of
the rushing future

The Horizon

the horizon line
divides a stanza
above of red lusty light

from the stanza below of
calm slumbering dream
we are rising from

Every Now and Then
for Brian & Kristine Jobe

every now and then
a lovely phrase that
every now is then but then

there comes a time when the sun
reveals that then is
now and ever shall be

The Resistance

how is it that i
live in paradise
the paradise of the now

when all around me the night
resists surrender
to the rising sun

Sunrise

sunrise begins to
last till sunset this
time of year and the days flash

over the lake like wild geese
honking frantically
in the meager light

About the Poet

Photo by Natalie Waters

Jonathan Potter is the author of *House of Words* (Korrektiv Press, 2010), *Tulips for Elsie* (Korrektiv Press, 2021), *Sunrise Yin* and *Sunrise Yang* (Korrektiv Press, 2022), and *How to Move to Canada* (Potstack Press, 2024). He divides his time between Washington (the state) and Montreal (the island).

A Note on the Type

The text of this book is set in Didot.
The Didot family played
a significant role
in the development of printing
over several generations,
beginning in the early 18th century in France.
François Didot was a Parisian merchant
who founded a bookstore in 1713
and received a printer's charter in 1754.
His son, François-Ambroise Didot,
succeeded him and made significant
contributions to printing technology,
including the invention of
the Didot point system,
a method for sizing typefaces
that became standard in Europe.

Acknowledgements & Apologies

With the exception of "The Shooter" (which appeared in the March 2, 2023 issue of *The Inlander*) most of the poems that inhabit this book originally appeared in *Potter Poems: Poetry in Process* – the Substack poetry newsletter I started in 2023.

A vibrant community of readers and writers exists across Substack, and I've tried to acknowledge the collaborative encouragement of individuals from that realm and other realms by dedicating individual poems in these pages to them/you. If I left you out (or someone you love) and you/they feel snubbed, please contact me and I will, if at all possible, add a dedication to you/them in a future edition of the book. By the same token, if you don't like your name appearing here, please forgive me! Let me know, and I will remove your name from future editions.

Special thanks are due to Patris for suggesting the title, to Martin Mc Carthy, Brian Jobe, and X. P. Callahan for editorial input, to Matt and Ron for beanhouse brotherhood, and to Mike Speriosu and Jed Moffit for moral support and donuts.

Jonathan Potter
June 1, 2025

Index of Titles

Above a House, 310
Above the River, 581
Accidental Companions, 460
Acknowledgement and Resolution, 445
After Seven Days, 462
Alchemy Of, The, 612
All Eyes on the Sunrise, 8
All Obstacles Dissolve in Time, 593
Although I Did Make It Out of Bed, 470
America, 53
Anecdote of the Stats, 265
Another Year, 331
Approach, 308
Aquamarine Jewel Sun, 339
As Any Animal Must Know, 399
As One Word Follows Another, 533
At Six O'Clock in the Morning, 604
Autumn River Sunrise Triptych, 474
Bad Blood, 229
Bailiwick of the Broken Light, The, 7
Ballad of Franz and Hank, The, 435
Bang! Bang! the Drum! 352
Bare Ruined Limbs, The, 273
Beware, 18
Beyond Our Fingertips, 15
BHV6539, 66
Birds and I, The, 121
Birds Were Whooping It Up, The, 57
Birdsong of Day, The, 118
Blazers, The, 646

Blue of the Sky, The, 181
Blurbs, 144
Border Closure, The, 547
Born to Be Borne, 575
Broken Limbs, The, 473
Broken Line in the Sky, The, 639
Burning Sky, The, 305
Burns Night Revisited, 542
Catching an Early Morning Flight, 469
Change in the First Line, The, 457
Charged with Change, 45
Chicago, 383
Children, 322
Chris Cook, 354
Clarity and Mystery of Love, The, 212
Clinging Like Fire, 301
Cold Ground, The, 402
Collapse of Night, The, 285
Color of Morning, The, 454
Columbia and the Yakima, The, 31
Columbia Park, 108
Common Loons, 251
Conclave of Trees, A, 195
Conçues pour Savourer la Vie, 30
Connective Tissue, 312
Continental Divide, The, 434
Continuity of Sky, The, 328
Courage to Radically Change, 490
Courtside, 378
Coyote Fellowship, The, 113
Creative, The, 6

Daily Sunrise, 69
Dark Dawn, The, 22
Dark Glow, 303
Dark Roast, 13
Dawn Came Down Like Dust, 514
Dawn Come Round Again, The, 28
Dawn Repairs the Damage, 157
Days Lining Up Like Birds, The, 574
Dear People of the River, 602
Dear Reader, 133
Dig, The, 480
Dignity of the Morning, The, 627
Dismal Winter, The, 24
Do You Believe in Magic? 396
Do You Know What It Means, 247
Dog & Horse Dream, 320
Dream of a Bob Dylan Seminar, 607
Dream of Bob Dylan Preaching, 610
Dream of Father Paschal and the Fries, 96
Dream of Going Back to College, 576
Dream of Hang Gliding with My Mother, 623
Dream of Jess and Sherman, 176
Dream of John Updike at the County Fair, 213
Dream of Mingling at a Conference, 452
Dream of My Daughter & My Two Cousins, 426
Dream of Peeing My Pants, 220

667

Dream of Sedation, 481
Dream of Skyboarding with Todd 100
Dream of Sleep-Driving, 240
Dream of the Biology Speech, 648
Dream of the Couch, 4
Dream of the Doctor and the Mask, 376
Dream of the Donald at Doggy Daycare, 442
Dream of the Intrusive Stoner, 436
Dream of the Kitchen Herb Garden, 196
Dream of the Rap Star Murder Case, 204
Dream of the Red Tin Box, 142
Dream of the Toaster & the Armed Women, 512
Dream of Vacation Skydiving, 170
Duality, The, 244
Duration of the Sunrise, The, 329
Each Person Is a Genius, 381
Early Morning Traffic, 106
Early This Morning 534
East Pasco, 47
Electric Lightbulb Standing in for the Sun, 382
Escape, 362
Every Now and Then, 656
Everything Happens, 48
Faced with a Gray Sky, 74
Farewell Song to Summer, 239
Favorable Outlook, A, 637
Feasts of Others, The, 269
Feverish Sky, 238
Figgate Burn, The, 295

Fingernail Moon, 184
Fire of the Earth Flames Up, The, 112
Fishing for Truth, 298
Flock of Words, A, 117
Fog Again, The, 338
Fog Refused to Lift, The, 472
Fogbound, 51
Fogbound at Day's Dawn, 438
Frog's Departure, 585
From Deep in the Dresser, 140
Frozen River, The, 640
Future Sunrise Will Come, A, 408
Garrulous Serious October, 555
Gazing into the Suburban Fog at Sunrise, 429
Gently Falling Rain, The, 483
Glassy River, The, 506
Globe Willow, The, 159
Glory of the Sun Decreases, The, 420
God Is a Train Car Graffiti Artist, 494
God Made Me a Rambling Man, 573
Going Back to When, 222
Gongoozling Along, 283
Good Day to Fly, A, 54
Good Morning, 179
Grace of Tire Tracks, The, 72
Grandmother, The, 482
Great Reset, The, 489
Grizzled the Morning, 475
Gulls Have Gathered, The, 198
Haiku Epitaph, 598
Half the Books in My Library, 422

Halfway to Halfway, 183
Hanging Fire Like an Old Suit, 302
Harbormaster, The, 511
High Beams in the Rain, 253
High Drive's Your Best Bet, 536
Hills West Above the Fog, 214
Honor Song for Death's Death, 10
Horizon Hidden, 81
Horizon, The, 655
Houses Made of Stone, 227
I Could Spend My Life Along the River, 615
I Don't Exist, 252
I Dreamt of My Father Last Night, 359
I Get off the Bus, 5
I Had My Time in the Past 149
I Have Known These Trees, 465
I Recall My Friend, 210
I Recall What I Forget, 344
I Thought Back, 209
I Walk Along the Canal, 99
I Was a Lineman, 503
I Woke in a Fit of Dark Unease, 349
I Woke in a Fog, 466
I Woke This Morning, 152
I Woke to My Heart Fluttering, 407
If Tomorrow Never Comes, 147
In Magical ink, 504
In Retreat from the Night, 335
In the Beginning, 508
In the Light of the Sun's Rising, 372
Inflation, 206
Innocence, 248

Innocent Clouds Obstruct the View, 400
Inwardly Free of Sorrow, 553
It Furthers, 330
It's Not a Matter of Flying, 632
Its Destiny, 288
Jeanie Elizabeth, 390
Jesus in 1920, 182
Jettisoning, 421
Just Beyond, 16
Just When I Thought, 191
Karen Mobley, 353
Leaves of the Last Day of June, 148
Let's Let Them Dance, 64
Lever du Soleil, 599
Lighthouse, 223
Like Beachcombing at Low Tide, 77
Like the Invisible Sun, 371
Like Water and Light, 261
Lone Wood Duck Before the Waves, The, 627
Long Has Winter Had Its Way, 175
Long-Distance Love Song, 538
Looking, 82
Looking East and West, 46
Los Angeles, 560
Love Is Strong, 351
Lowly Street, The, 70
Manic Sapphic, 554
Manuscript, 257
Meditation, 526
Milkmaid, 124
Mind of William Butler Yeats, The, 263
Mississippi, The, 215
Molting, 492
Mom, 126
Mon Amour and I, 311
Montana, 337

Montreal Winter Sunrise Scene, 58
Moon Reflects the Unseen Sun, The, 525
Moon That Rose, The, 361
Moon, The, 416
Moon This Morning, The, 486
Morning Chill, The, 52
Morning Creeps In, The, 597
Morning Is Like a Cat, The, 636
Mountains East of Bozeman Town, The, 513
Moving Shadows on the Grass, 92
Museum of the Eternal Now, 601
My Fifty-Ninth Birthday, 286
My First Step, 350
My Hometown Enduring, 332
My Inner Rehab Project, 236
My Lady of My River Dreams 545
My Long Travel Day, 541
My Nine Lives, 516
My Poetry 374
My Treasure Chest of Old Journals, 479
My Vision Is Set Ablaze, 259
My Wife, 151
Nance Van Winckel, 355
Near the Confluence, 638
Nearing Completion, 643
New Orleans Deluge, 306
New Orleans Sestina, 594
New Orleans, 274
Nine Dawns, 393

Nine in the Fourth Place, 137
Not Too Hard but Hard Enough, 78
Nothing, The, 21
O River of My Childhood Longings Lost, 38
Ode to Ayr, 185
On a Gravel Road, 186
On the Cable Bridge, 193
On the Cusp, 114
On the Train Platform, 87
One and All, 116
One Moment, The, 336
Open Field, The, 499
Ordinary Day Begins, An, 327
Oratory, The, 346
Our New Agenda, 249
Outskirts of Town at Dawn, The, 341
Parable of the Tangled Lamb, The, 224
Past the Halfway Point, 590
Path Forward, The, 258
Pettiness of Pathetically Underpaid Poets, The, 546
Phantom Sunrise, 476
Pines, The, 527
Pink and Black and Blue, 39
Place You Find Yourself, The, 528
Playground of the Wind, 189
Poetry on the Great Prose Plains, 125
Ponderosa, The, 500
Preparing for an Interview, 635
Psalm, A, 272
Qualchan Came to See Me, 160
Ragged Ridges, 345
Rain Falling on the River, 493

Rain This Morning Falling, The, 150
Rain This Morning, The, 65
Reading of the Sky, The, 458
Recalling Times I Never Knew, 262
Red Glow, The, 19
Refugees of Morning, 450
Remedy, The, 363
Repetition, The, 153
Resistance, The, 657
Riding Backwards on a Train, 495
Riding My Bike to the Library in the Rain, 568
River and the Sky, The, 71
River Consolation, 37
River Graffiti, 485
River Rover, The, 293
Road Kill 373
Roof Beam Is About to Fall, The, 284
Roulette Wheel of Life's Changes, The, 567
RSVP, 111
Saffron Blackberry Sunrise, 644
Sandhill Cranes in the Morning, 123
Sapphic Psalm, 40
Saturday Director's Cut, 202
Scene is Set, The, 1
Scraps, 294
Season of the Change-Up, The, 491
Seattle, 162
September Is the Month, 131
Shade Is Pulled, The, 318
Shakespeare, Too, 522
Shooter, The, 296
Sick Day, 219
Sign, 89
Six Haiku at Sunrise, 515
Skies Cleared Over London, The, 552
Sky at First Glance, The, 304
Sky Is Crazy With Swallows, The, 559
Sky Is Like My Beloved, The, 17
Sky This Morning, The,
Slit of Serious Sunrise, A, 415
Slow and Steady Sun, The, 548
Smoke from Fires All Around Us, The, 375
Snafu, 158
Solstice Weather, 201
Something Like the Sunrise, 233
Song to the Ocean, 596
Southbound Train, 237
Spring Morning Progression, 461
Squirrel Sestina, 412
Squirrels, The, 629
St. Joseph's Crutches, 287
Still Asleep I Leap, 654
Still We Breathe, 90
Streets Are Sheets of Ice, 264
Struggle of the Sun to Rise, The, 414
Struggling Sun Well-Risen, The, 451
Substack Haiku Sequence, 342
Sun Above, the Sun Below, The, 582
Sun Behind Mountains, 228
Sun Came Out, The, 235
Sun Gives Birth to Itself, The, 33
Sunday Morning Coming Down, 107
Sunrise, 658
Sunrise and I, The, 254
Sunrise Behind Pines, 403
Sunrise Filtered Through the Mist, 600
Sunrise from My Bedroom Window, 130
Sunrise from the Rose, 340
Sunrise Ghazal, 430
Sunrise in the Morning Mist, 250
Sunrise Like a Coffee Stain, The, 132
Sunrise Mostly Hidden, The, 80
Sunrise on the Firth, 586
Sunrise on the Land Beyond, The, 367
Sunrise Solo Sestina, 630
Sunrise Through the Sagebrush, 529
Sunrise Wooing, 316
Sunset Sonnet, 319
Superior Sunrise, 317
Swallow Sunrise, 194
Sweet Spot in the Chaos, The, 95
Syllabically, 154
Take a Deep Breath, 192
Taking the Long View, 530
That Fragment Reflected, 441
Their Silver Noses, 73
Then One Morning You Wake Up, 11
There Can Be No Why, 521
There Is No Was, 297
There May Be an Ideal Lake, 589
These Messages, 190
These Times We're Living In, 105
Thinking Back to Playing Soccer, 63
Thirteen Ways of Looking at the Sunrise, 364

This Canal Is a Poet, 270
This Is How, 88
This Morning Was a Long Time Ago, 234
This Morning's Version of the Sunrise, 401
This Morning's Waking, 360
This Poem, for Example, 129
This River Brings Time, 507
This Sunrise, 134
This Work, 459
Three Surreal Haiku, 584
Tina Turner, 29
To Increase Is to Decrease, 419
Toward the Sea, 292
Travel Day, 27
Travis Laurence Naught, 352
Treachery of the Sun, The, 551
Treading on the Tail of a Tiger, 85
Triolet From Memory, A, 260
True Affection, 446
Tugboats and Bridges and Sleepy Eyes, 180
Twenty-Third Psalm, The, 122
Unburning Bush, The, 428
Upstream, 44
Variations on a Squirrel, 410
Vienna, 616
Waiting, 43
Waking in the Dark, 86
Waking Mornings, 32
Walking on Water, Holding Fire, 645
Was I the Sun or the River, 315
Way, The, 324
Weight of the Sky, The, 404
What Molecules Move, 484
What Is This For? 496
What Time It Is Where You Are, 138
Whatever Progress I Made, 425
When Deliverance Comes, 409
When I Arrived in Spokane, 433
When It Snowed in New Orleans, 449
Where Not To, 607
Where You Are Flying, 266
Wherever My Father Went, 291
Whisky-Coloured Glow, 169
Whisper of Words, A, 139
Why, 647
Windy Morning on the River, A, 603
With Whom Am I Speaking? 110
World Inside You, The, 556
You, 20

www.ingramcontent.com/pod-product-compliance
Lightning Source LLC
Chambersburg PA
CBHW060357230426
43663CB00008B/1299